Februar

33 1/3 Global

33 1/3 Global, a series related to but independent from **33 1/3**, takes the format of the original series of short, music-based books and brings the focus to music throughout the world. With initial volumes focusing on Japanese and Brazilian music, the series will also include volumes on the popular music of Australia/Oceania, Europe, Africa, the Middle East, and more.

33 1/3 Japan

Series Editor: Noriko Manabe

Spanning a range of artists and genres—from the 1970s rock of Happy End to technopop band Yellow Magic Orchestra, the Shibuya-kei of Cornelius, classic anime series *Cowboy Bebop*, J-Pop/EDM hybrid Perfume, and vocaloid star Hatsune Miku—**33 1/3 Japan** is a series devoted to in-depth examination of Japanese popular music of the twentieth and twenty-first centuries.

Published Titles:

Supercell's *Supercell* by Keisuke Yamada

AKB48 by Patrick W. Galbraith and Jason G. Karlin

Yoko Kanno's *Cowboy Bebop Soundtrack* by Rose Bridges

Perfume's *Game* by Patrick St. Michel

Cornelius's *Fantasma* by Martin Roberts

Joe Hisaishi's *My Neighbor Totoro: Soundtrack* by Kunio Hara

Shonen Knife's *Happy Hour* by Brooke McCorkle

Nenes' *Koza Dabasa* by Henry Johnson

Yuming's *The 14th Moon* by Lasse Lehtonen

Toshiko Akiyoshi-Lew Tabackin Big Band's *Kogun* by E. Taylor Atkins

S.O.B.'s *Don't Be Swindle* by Mahon Murphy and Ran Zwigenberg

Forthcoming Titles:

Kohaku Utagassen: The Red and White Song Contest by Shelley Brunt

Yellow Magic Orchestra's *Yellow Magic Orchestra* by Toshiyuki Ohwada

33 1/3 Brazil

Series Editor: Jason Stanyek

Covering the genres of samba, tropicália, rock, hip hop, forró, bossa nova, heavy metal and funk, among others, **33 1/3 Brazil** is a series devoted to in-depth examination of the most important Brazilian albums of the twentieth and twenty-first centuries.

Published Titles:

Caetano Veloso's *A Foreign Sound* by Barbara Browning

Tim Maia's *Tim Maia Racional Vols. 1 &2* by Allen Thayer

João Gilberto and Stan Getz's *Getz/Gilberto* by Brian McCann

Gilberto Gil's *Refazenda* by Marc A. Hertzman

Dona Ivone Lara's *Sorriso Negro* by Mila Burns

Milton Nascimento and Lô Borges's *The Corner Club* by Jonathon Grasse

Racionais MCs' *Sobrevivendo no Inferno* by Derek Pardue

Naná Vasconcelos's *Saudades* by Daniel B. Sharp

Chico Buarque's First *Chico Buarque* by Charles A. Perrone

Forthcoming titles:

Jorge Ben Jor's *África Brasil* by Frederick J. Moehn

33 1/3 Europe

Series Editor: Fabian Holt

Spanning a range of artists and genres, **33 1/3 Europe** offers engaging accounts of popular and culturally significant albums of Continental Europe and the North Atlantic from the twentieth and twenty-first centuries.

Published Titles:

Darkthrone's *A Blaze in the Northern Sky* by Ross Hagen
Ivo Papazov's *Balkanology* by Carol Silverman
Heiner Müller and Heiner Goebbels's *Wolokolamsker Chaussee* by Philip V. Bohlman
Modeselektor's *Happy Birthday!* by Sean Nye
Mercyful Fate's *Don't Break the Oath* by Henrik Marstal
Bea Playa's *I'll Be Your Plaything* by Anna Szemere and András Rónai
Various Artists' *DJs do Guetto* by Richard Elliott
Czesław Niemen's *Niemen Enigmatic* by Ewa Mazierska and Mariusz Gradowski
Massada's *Astaganaga* by Lutgard Mutsaers
Los Rodriguez's *Sin Documentos* by Fernán del Val and Héctor Fouce
Édith Piaf's *Récital 1961* by David Looseley
Nuovo Canzoniere Italiano's *Bella Ciao* by Jacopo Tomatis
Iannis Xenakis's *Persepolis* by Aram Yardumian
Vopli Vidopliassova's *Tantsi* by Maria Sonevytsky
Amália Rodrigues's *Amália at the Olympia* by Lila Ellen Gray
Ardit Gjebrea's *Projekt Jon* by Nicholas Tochka
Aqua's *Aquarium* by C.C. McKee
J.M.K.E.'s *To the Cold Land* by Brigitta Davidjants
Taco Hemingway's *Jarmark* by Kamila Rymajdo
Einstürzende Neubauten's *Kollaps* by Melle Jan Kromhout and Jan Nieuwenhuis
CCCP - FEDELI ALLA LINEA's *Affinità - Divergenze Fra il Compagno Togliatti e Noi* by Giacomo Bottà
Silly's *Februar* by Michael Rauhut

Forthcoming Titles:

Sigur Rós' *Ágætis Byrjun* by Tore Størvold

Aphrodite's Child's *666* by Ana Leorne

33 1/3 Oceania

Series Editors: Jon Stratton (senior editor) and Jon Dale (specializing in books on albums from Aotearoa/New Zealand)

Spanning a range of artists and genres from Australian Indigenous artists to Maori and Pasifika artists, from Aotearoa/New Zealand noise music to Australian rock, and including music from Papua and other Pacific islands, **33 1/3 Oceania** offers exciting accounts of albums that illustrate the wide range of music made in the Oceania region.

Published Titles:

John Farnham's *Whispering Jack* by Graeme Turner

The Church's *Starfish* by Chris Gibson

Regurgitator's *Unit* by Lachlan Goold and Lauren Istvandity

Kylie Minogue's *Kylie* by Adrian Renzo and Liz Giuffre

Alastair Riddell's *Space Waltz* by Ian Chapman

Hunters & Collectors's *Human Frailty* by Jon Stratton

The Front Lawn's *Songs from the Front Lawn* by Matthew Bannister

Bic Runga's *Drive* by Henry Johnson

The Dead C's *Clyma est mort* by Darren Jorgensen

Ed Kuepper's *Honey Steel's Gold* by John Encarnacao

Chain's *Toward the Blues* by Peter Beilharz

Hilltop Hoods' *The Calling* by Dianne Rodger

Screamfeeder's *Kitten Licks* by Ben Green and Ian Rogers

The Clean's *Boodle Boodle Boodle* by Geoff Stahl

The Avalanches' *Since I Left You* by Charles Fairchild

John Sangster's *Lord of the Rings Vols. 1-3* by Bruce Johnson

Soundtrack from *Saturday Night Fever* by Clinton Walker

Eyeliner's *BUY NOW* by Michael Brown

TISM's *Machiavelli and the Four Seasons* by Tyler Jenke

Crowded House's *Together Alone* by Barnaby Smith

silverchair's *Frogstomp* by Jay Daniel Thompson

Various Artists' *Truckload of Sky: The Lost Songs of David McComb* by Glenn D'Cruz

Robert Forster's *Danger in the Past* by Patrick Chapman

Tame Impala's *Currents* by Alister Newstead

Forthcoming Titles:

The Triffids' *Born Sandy Devotional* by Christina Ballico

5MMM's *Compilation Album of Adelaide Bands 1980* by Collette Snowden

INXS' *Kick* by Lauren Moxey

Sunnyboys' *Sunnyboys* by Stephen Bruel

The La De Das' *The Happy Prince* by John Tebbutt

Gary Shearston's *Dingo* by Peter Mills

Kate Ceberano's *Brave* by Panizza Allmark

Dinah Lee's *Introducing Dinah Lee* by Kimberly Cannady

The Waifs' *Up All Night* by Rebecca Bennison

The Three Out's *Move* by James Gaunt

Split Enz' *Mental Notes* by Michael Lamb

Douglas Lilburn's *Complete Electro-Acoustic Works* by Bruce Russell

Savage Garden's *Affirmation* by Pat O'Grady

Dick Diver's *Calendar Days* by Mitch Ryan

33 1/3 South Asia

Series Editor: Natalie Sarrazin

From the films of Bollywood and Lollywood, to home-grown *bhangra* hip-hop, Hindu devotional pop and Sufi rock, Sri Lankan rap, Indo jazz and disco, new-wave electronica and diasporic Asian Underground scene, **33 1/3 South Asia** takes readers on a sonically diverse journey through the most significant soundtracks and albums from the twentieth and twenty-first centuries.

Published:

Dil Chahta Hai Soundtrack by Jayson Beaster-Jones

Lata Mangeshkar's *My Favourites, Volume 2* by Anirudha Bhattacharjee and Chandrashekhar Rao

Coke Studio (Season 14) by Rakae Rehman Jamil and Khadija Muzaffar

33 1/3 Africa

Series Editor: Michael Veal

33 1/3 Africa is a series of books on canonical, album-length works of African music including traditional music, experimental music, and, with particular emphasis, popular music. Academic and journalistic writing results in sophisticated, nuanced and accessible narratives on African music.

Published:

Fela Anikulapo-Kuti's *Sorrow Tears and Blood* by Stephanie Shonekan

Forthcoming Titles:

Cesária Évora's *Miss Perfumado* by Jacqueline Georgis

Paul Simon's *Graceland* by Kalvin Schmidt-Rimpler Dinh

Nico, Rochereau, Roger & L'African Fiesta - *Volume 1 (1962-1963)* by Frank Gunderson

Februar

Michael Rauhut

Translated from the German
by Noah Harley

Series Editor: Fabian Holt

BLOOMSBURY ACADEMIC
NEW YORK • LONDON • OXFORD • NEW DELHI • SYDNEY

BLOOMSBURY ACADEMIC
Bloomsbury Publishing Inc, 1359 Broadway, New York, NY 10018, USA
Bloomsbury Publishing Plc, 50 Bedford Square, London, WC1B 3DP, UK
Bloomsbury Publishing Ireland, 29 Earlsfort Terrace, Dublin 2, D02 AY28, Ireland

BLOOMSBURY, BLOOMSBURY ACADEMIC and the Diana logo are trademarks of Bloomsbury Publishing Plc

First published in the United States of America 2026

Library of Congress Cataloging-in-Publication Data

Names: Rauhut, Michael, 1963- author
Title: Februar / Michael Rauhut.
Description: [1]. | New York, NY : Bloomsbury Academic, 2026. | Series: 33 1/3 Europe | Includes bibliographical references and index. | Summary: "To this day, Silly continues to be one of Germany's most influential and successful rock acts. Written in close collaboration with the masterminds of Silly, this account is based on a wealth of never before published archival documents and in contradiction of clichés around socialist state propaganda. It captures the fundamental political changes, the collapse of socialism in Eastern Europe, and illustrates the global interconnectedness in rock. This is a thrilling and analytical story of the creation and impact of a record that may still provide food for thought for the debate about the ties between East German identity and popular music today"– Provided by publisher.
Identifiers: LCCN 2025029022 | ISBN 9798765109304 hardback | ISBN 9798765109311 paperback | ISBN 9798765109335 pdf | ISBN 9798765109328 epub
Subjects: LCSH: Silly (Musical group) Februar | Rock music–Germany (East)–History and criticism
Classification: LCC ML421.S523 R38 2026 | DDC 782.42166092/2–dc23/eng/20251209
LC record available at https://lccn.loc.gov/2025029022

ISBN: HB: 979-8-7651-0930-4
PB: 979-8-7651-0931-1
ePDF: 979-8-7651-0933-5
eBook: 979-8-7651-0932-8

Series: 33 1/3 Europe

Typeset by Deanta Global Publishing Services, Chennai, India
Printed and bound in the United States of America

For product safety related questions contact productsafety@bloomsbury.com.

To find out more about our authors and books visit www.bloomsbury.com and sign up for our newsletters.

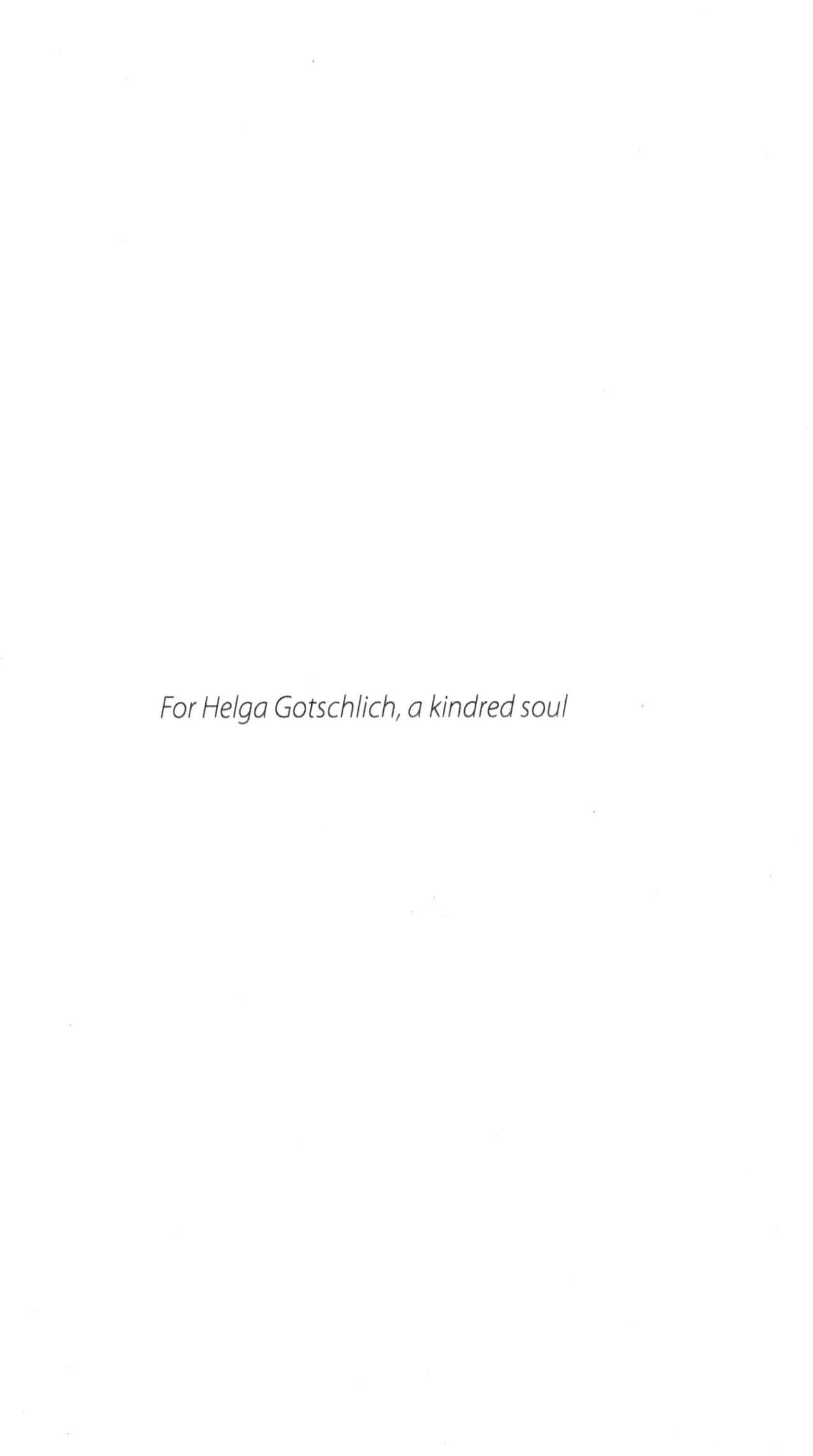

For Helga Gotschlich, a kindred soul

Birds of paradise can't be kept caged
They need all the sky up above
Just one part is too small.

—"PARADIESVÖGEL" (BIRDS OF PARADISE), SILLY

Contents

Figures

Abbreviations

A	arrangement
ac	acoustic
ADN	Allgemeiner Deutscher Nachrichtendienst [General German News Service; state news agency in the GDR]
ARD	Arbeitsgemeinschaft der öffentlich-rechtlichen Rundfunkanstalten der Bundesrepublik Deutschland [Consortium of Public-Service Broadcasters in the Federal Republic of Germany]
arr	arrangement
BArch	Bundesarchiv [Federal Archive]
bg	bass guitar
BMG	Bertelsmann Music Group
BRD	Bundesrepublik Deutschland [Federal Republic of Germany (West Germany)]
CBS	Columbia Broadcasting System
CD	compact disc
comp	composition
c/w	coupled with

DDR Deutsche Demokratische Republik [German Democratic Republic (East Germany)]

DNA Deoxyribonucleic Acid

DRA Deutsches Rundfunkarchiv [German Broadcasting Archive]

dr drums

DSB Deutsche Schallplatten Berlin [record company]

FDJ Freie Deutsche Jugend [Free German Youth; East German communist youth organization]

g guitar

GmbH Gesellschaft mit beschränkter Haftung [limited liability company]

IM Inoffizieller Mitarbeiter [unofficial Stasi collaborator]

K Komposition [composition]

keyb keyboards

ld leader

LP long-playing record

MIDI Musical Instrument Digital Interface

Mitropa Mitteleuropäische Schlaf- und Speisewagen-Aktiengesellschaft [Central European Sleeping and Dining Cars Incorporated] (largely used as an abbreviation for train station restaurants in the GDR)

MfS Ministerium für Staatssicherheit [Ministry for State Security]

org organ

p piano

PA public address system

perc percussion

PR public relations

RIAS Rundfunk im amerikanischen Sektor [Radio in the American Sector]

SED Sozialistische Einheitspartei Deutschlands [Socialist Unity Party of Germany]

SMPTE Society of Motion Picture and Television Engineers

Stasi Staatssicherheitsdienst der DDR [East German state security service]

syn synthesizer

T Text [lyrics]

TV television

USA United States of America

v violin

VEB Volkseigener Betrieb [state owned enterprise]

voc vocals

ZK Zentralkomitee [Central Committee]

Silly—Februar
Amiga 856316

Side A

1. Ein Gespenst geht um [A Specter Haunts] (4:05)
   T: Gundermann/Danz
   K: Barton/Danz
   A: Silly/Hoffmann

2. Verlorene Kinder [Lost Children] (4:19)
   T: Gundermann/Danz
   K: Barton/Danz
   A: Silly

3. Alle gegen einen [All Against One] (3:52)
   T: Gundermann/Danz
   K: Hassbecker/Barton/Danz
   A: Silly

4. SOS (3:39)
   T: Gundermann/Danz
   K: Hassbecker/Danz
   A: Silly/Hoffmann

5. Über ihr taute das Eis [Above Her The Ice Set to Thaw] (5:26)
T: Karma
K: Hassbecker/Danz
A: Silly

Side B

1. Traumteufel [Dream Devil] (3:43)
T: Gundermann/Danz
K: Barton/Danz
A: Silly

2. Landekreuz auf meiner Seele [Touchdown on my Soul] (4:20)
T: Gundermann/Danz
K: Barton/Danz
A: Silly

3. Alles wird besser [It's All Getting Better] (4:15)
T: Karma
K: Hassbecker/Danz
A: Silly

4. Männer wollen Frauen [Men Want Women] (4:04)
T: Gundermann/Danz
K: Hassbecker/Danz
A: Silly/Hoffmann

5. Paradiesvögel [Birds of Paradise] (3:40)
T: Gundermann/Danz
K: Barton/Danz
A: Silly/Hoffmann

Silly: Ritchie Barton (syn, p, hammond org, voc)
Uwe Hassbecker (g, solo g, ac g, v)
Jäcki Reznicek (fretless bg)
Herbert Junck (dr, perc)
Thomas Fritzsching (g)
Tamara Danz (voc)

Uwe Hoffmann (computer programming, perc)

Horn Arrangements: Uwe Hoffmann & Ritchie Barton
Choral Arrangements: Tamara Danz
String Arrangements for Track 2, Side A: Uwe Hoffmann & Ritchie Barton
Backing Vocals: Thomas Hein, Tamara Danz, Ritchie Barton, Uwe Hoffmann, Uwe Hassbecker, Ronny Schreinzer, Jäcki Reznicek, Dieter Ortlepp

Produced in 1988, released in 1989

Produced by Uwe Hoffmann
Recording Engineer: David Heilmann
Assistant: Dieter Ortlepp
Mixed by Uwe Hoffmann & David Heilmann

Editor: René Büttner
Promotion Design and Campaign: Marcus-Macchio-Produktion Berlin
Graphic Design: Jürgen Schmidt-André

A co-production of VEB Deutsche Schallplatten, Berlin/GDR and BMG Ariola Munich/BRD
Recorded and mixed at Preußen Tonstudio (West Berlin)

Lyrics printed on the inner sleeve

Acknowledgments

A project like this always entails a period of intense deeply felt encounters. I'm obliged to a host of friends and colleagues who shared my enthusiasm and clambered down into the time machine with me. I'll never forget the day in September 2023 when the musicians from Silly invited me into their studio. We were listening to *Februar* together, discussing details related to its composition and production. With an unspoken gesture, Ritchie, Uwe, and Jäcki each picked up their instruments to accompany the powerful sound emanating from the speakers, transported themselves. It was a moment that went deep under the skin. Subsequently, whenever I asked the three for information or material, whether in one of our many meetings, by telephone, or by email, they responded selflessly and patiently. We often wish our heroes not only to be first-rate artists but good people. I always had the feeling that here the two were combined.

My sincere thanks also go to those I interviewed, Tamara Danz, David Heilmann, Christian Hentschel, Uwe Hoffmann, Werner Karma, Dieter Ortlepp, Jim Rakete, and Thomas Stein; the photographers Ute Mahler, Karin Rocholl, Gabriele Senft, Ulrich Burchert, Herbert Schulze, Jürgen Sieker, and Rolf Zoellner; graphic designer Jürgen Schmidt-André; Conny Gundermann, Gabriele Erber, Yvonne Omsen, Beate Peter, Anke Weiße, Jürgen Balitzki, Ingolv Haaland, Fabian Holt, Gunther Krex, Reinhard

Lorenz, Martin Pfleiderer, Rolf Rische, and Peter Wicke for their expert counsel and wholehearted support. Noah Harley for his devoted translation, and Patricia Anne Simpson and Elisabeth Lauffer for their careful reading; the Faculty of Fine Arts at the University of Agder in Kristiansand, Norway for financial support; Marion and Jürgen Barth, Carola Borgwardt-Mewes and Jörg Borgwardt, Katja Franke and Claus Ungerechts, Eva-Maria and Svein Jordbrudal, Jens-Christian Katzschner, Ragnhild Nilsen and Michael Schulte, and especially Helga Gotschlich, Marina Zollmann, and Detlef Siegfried for their enduring friendship. Who would I be without them? Finally, I am deeply bound to Birgit, Lily, and Markus, my family.

1 Before the Needle Drops

A Masterpiece, and a Sign of the Times

It's September 15, 1989, the air heavy with anticipation at the Silly concert in Altdöbern, a village out in the East German provinces. Lead singer Tamara Danz steps up to the mic to address the fans. Times are hard, summer giving way to a harvest of doubts. In the past two months, over fifty thousand people have fled East Germany's Socialist state for the West, more than ever before. It feels as though the country is bleeding itself dry. What's next? Will it be the "last one to leave please turn out the light," fulfilling the macabre saying? Will a "Chinese solution" quash all resistance with armed force? Is the state ready for reform, will the government change? Or—the option nobody thinks possible—might the Wall even come down? Tamara Danz's words ring out, encouraging the crowd to remain in the GDR, cautioning against lethargy, demanding political change. The people listen, enthralled, before thundering their applause, celebrating a moment of hope and shared belonging. Stasi henchmen line the edge of the stage in a silent show of power. Eight weeks later, the GDR falls like a house of cards.

I've known Silly since their early days and seen them live any number of times, whether in student clubs, cultural centers, or the Palast der Republik in East Berlin. Yet that night remains stuck in my memory. It revealed the true essence of the group beneath the glitzy surface—the commercial success, pitch-perfect sound, and immaculate style. At the band's core lay the musicians' restlessness, their perpetual drive toward risk and change. That attitude ran like a leitmotif throughout the band's history, putting them in a league of their own among GDR acts. For Silly, rock music was never simply about entertainment or making a living—it was a statement, a way of showing where you stood. That came through most forcefully in the lyrics, which rendered everyday life in East Germany in poetic images, met conflicts in society head on, and posed the existential questions that state-controlled discourse conveniently managed to miss. Silly were a definitively political band.

Yet the band's restlessness, their unbroken will to reinvent themselves, was reflected just as clearly in the innovative force of their music, which took new form with every passing album. After an exploratory phase luring crowds out onto the dance floor with reggae and funk, Silly steered toward new wave, absorbing its energy and sensuality to fashion a musical language of their own. The same creative truck with international trends marked subsequent releases, with angular, challenging rock and ambitious pop providing the next accents. On *Februar*, their final GDR album, Silly took its inspiration from the digital age without coming across either as cold or kitsch. With each musical metamorphosis came a shift in the band's visual aesthetic, new styles of clothing and haircuts.

Februar represented the culmination of Silly's artistic output prior to the fall of the Wall. In an exquisite body of work, the album stands out in a number of regards, not just as an artistic masterpiece but an eloquent sign of the times. Released in early 1989, *Februar* anticipated the collapse of socialism by addressing the political erosion of Eastern Europe. Yet the record also provided powerful evidence for the complicated set of circumstances under which rock music existed in the GDR, a situation that the wooden propaganda of the state apparatus could hardly keep obscured. Contrary to what rash, black-and-white interpretations might suggest, the relationship between the East German state and rock was truly dynamic, defined by a host of contradictions, broad gray areas, and unrestricted zones—that, along with an ever-present divide between intention and reality.

Importantly, *Februar* also revealed the ways in which rock music's development in East Germany was embedded in a global context, Iron Curtain and Cold War political maneuvering notwithstanding. The fundamental impetus may have come from the West, but a certain feedback loop existed. As the only major coproduction between East and West Germany in the field of popular music, *Februar* revealed the outermost extremities that relationship could reach. Both camps, Amiga in the East and BMG Ariola in the West, declared the album a top priority; it was personally supervised by managing directors from both labels, came on the market in two versions, underwent different promotional campaigns, and elicited different responses. *Februar* encapsulates the divergent economic, social, and political significance that rock held in the East versus the West.

Whose Memories, Which History?

Research into East German rock has flourished since the fall of the Berlin Wall, with no end in sight. In state archives previously closed to the public, a store of data is now available that may be unique the world over for the comprehensive power of its testimony. Documents that were once confidential or secret have cast policy and everyday life in East Germany in an entirely new light, prompting thorough corrections to earlier visions of the past. Yet the sheer number of publications by authors the world over is hardly able to obscure the imbalances and shortcomings. The general emphasis lies with currents and phenomena in rock music that are ascribed overtly subversive potential, with prominent public profiles that lend them a certain exoticism into the present day; punk or heavy metal, the underground that positions itself as culturally alternative, even politically oppositional. The cultural mainstream by contrast, as was visible in GDR media, and had accommodated itself to the specific climate of East Germany, presents a much less dramatic image and draws only peripheral interest. It is hastily dismissed as overly affirmative or too close to the system—that, or is simply ignored in the misguided assumption that it cannot provide deeper insight into the mechanisms of power or true conflicts present in East German society.

The opposite is the case. Unlike the nonconformist underground that sought either to evade state clutches or rebel against them, successful bands in the GDR developed an artistic survival strategy of adapting to the circumstances while simultaneously looking to push the boundaries. Whether measured in terms of public acclaim, privileges, status, or success, Silly unquestionably belonged to the established mainstream in the GDR. Yet by inspiring a mass audience with subtle social critique and musical influences from outside the GDR, the band chipped away at the status quo more effectively than a handful of angry punks who may have howled their discontent unabashedly, true, but did so in quasi-private environments.

A band like Silly spells out the unique power that rock music held in socialism just as clearly as it does the specific conditions under which that music was produced and distributed. Unlike almost any other group, Silly's career lays bare the unrelenting tensions at play in negotiating with the state, and the maximum flexibility of the framework. The band's trajectory speaks to unsuspecting possibilities and border-crossings, and serves as a parable for the contradictions of the GDR. Silly's story is one of caprice and censorship, compromise and tactics, but it is also one of upstanding action. It is the story I would like to tell with this book. I portray *Februar* as the end result of a long process of emancipation that brought successively greater artistic and political leeway, delving into the complex biography of the band to do so.

A second shortcoming of GDR rock historiography is its ghettoization; though recognized as a field of research, it remains isolated within broader professional discourse. The same applies not just where (patently anglocentric) global histories are concerned, but for conversations within Germany as well. Since incorporating the East under its own rules in 1990, the West has looked on GDR rock as provincial, a form of music that bears the twin stigmas of repression and opportunism and is thus necessarily of lesser quality. The result is that it is either marginalized or ignored from the outset. Academic discourse as dictated by the West forces it to the periphery in the overall story of Germany. In anthologies that purport to cover both West and East, GDR rock often appears as a fig leaf, with a few catchphrases or chapters intended to give an impression of balance (see Rauhut and Peter 2021 for greater detail).

This antipathy is most glaring in the media's perception of GDR rock, which it tucks away under the pejorative heading of "Ost-Rock," or East Rock, excluding it from the canon. When *Musikexpress*, a major music journal, revealed its "100 Best German Albums" in 2019, a grand total of four GDR releases made it onto the bottom of the list—three records and one illegally produced underground cassette tape. Silly's epochal record *Mont Klamott* from 1983 took last place. Of the "500 Best Albums of All Time" worldwide as selected by *Rolling Stone Germany* in 2023, thirty-one came from West Germany and two from Austria, in addition to the debut of Nina Hagen, who had emigrated from East Berlin to the West a good year before the record was released. Of East German artists there was nary a peep. The disregard was all the more blatant given that the list wasn't limited to rock and pop but included jazz musicians, singer-songwriters, and world music acts. A glance at the fine print revealed the crux of the matter: with one or two exceptions, all 135 jurors had been socialized and conditioned in West Germany.

The results of the *Rolling Stone* critics' poll support the devastating conclusion that University of Leipzig literature professor Dirk Oschmann reaches in his 2023 book *Der Osten: Eine westdeutsche Erfindung* [The East: A West German Invention]. One of the year's most hotly debated works of political non-fiction, Oschmann finds that the experience of life in the GDR has gradually and diligently been scrubbed from media awareness. The "victors of history" have hermetically sealed off their system of rule; the public space "not only lies fully in West German hands, but is thoroughly dominated by West German perspectives, all things being equal" (Oschmann 2023, 30). In Oschmann's charged analysis, the West justifies its claim to interpretive supremacy by asserting its moral superiority, although in truth the effort has served profoundly undemocratic, merciless campaigns of repression conducted in a neo-colonial vein, a "total exclusion from social and economic policy" (ibid., 76 and 93).

Despite its sobering assessment, Oschmann's polemic, which joins a growing corpus on the fate of former East Germans in the process of reunification, also passionately attests to the resilience of identity. The arts constitute a special kind of forum for self-expression. The state can indeed raze cityscapes, remove monuments and symbols of past eras, or wipe recollection of the GDR from the media and school curricula—along with the critique of the present moment that springs from that recollection. What it cannot erase, however, are the traces of collective cultural memory as left behind in literature, visual art, or music.

In the early 1990s, after it seemed to lay buried forever beneath the wreckage of the Wall, GDR rock experienced a resurgence. The return of earlier acts and their hits took part in a general trend, as doubts and the remembrance of bygone values mixed in with the wave of euphoria unleashed by the market economy's promises of liberty for all. The West derided the unexpected turn as "Ostalgie"—a satirical portmanteau of sorts to denote nostalgia (*Nostalgie*) for the East (*Ost*)—at the same time peddling it for all it was worth. The title page on July 3, 1995, in *Der Spiegel* announced a new "Eastern feeling," glossing it as a form of "homesickness for the old order." The interpretation became standard going forward, yet it missed the main point. What had been described as a skewed vision of the past was in fact a reckoning with the present, a form of emancipation and "productive act of self-empowerment on the part of East Germans," who "took back the right they had relinquished and been deprived of—to interpret their own biographies" (Ahbe 1997, 619). True to their guiding principle of constant reinvention, Silly never fit into the set pattern of "Ostalgie." Yet the band's music and attitude retain clear traces of their origins to this day.

Sources and Perspectives

Confrontations with the past are always relative to the standpoint of the observer; her degree of involvement, proximity or distance, political motives, and the foil of the present will all confer particular accents to the final image. One might liken the subject-object relationship to how we view a building. Close up, details emerge—the bumpy patches, hairline cracks, and crumbling plaster, but also any filigree or ornamentation. Take a couple of steps back and the eye registers more complex structures, sensing the overall scope of the building, its construction and static equilibrium. Regardless of how she positions herself, the onlooker's image of the building will remain forever incomplete. Arriving at deeper historical understanding requires us to acknowledge different perspectives and balance out the tensions that exist between them discursively (Covach 2020, 33).

My own perspective is twofold—I write as a researcher and an insider. It seems important to mention this since it sheds light on my motivations and points of access. I grew up in the GDR as a rock fan. I was a part of the scene, as familiar with daily routines as with the facets of the political system. The narrative I present here is tinged with personal experience. I realize that the language of the state apparatus can't be taken as the "whole truth," though I am equally wary of criticism of the same made from a safe distance. Historical images are the product of interpretation and remain fluid as a result. We only apprehend the past via our relationship to the present and visions of the future (Treitler 2001, 362). Our memories are inevitably shaped by prevailing power relationships (Green 2018, 212), as becomes only too clear when engaging with the history of the GDR and its legacy. Stigmatizing and disparaging the East, its mentality and culture, also devalues its rock music. Yet that music had tremendous power as a means of communication and as a social engine and was constantly questioning the conditions of life in the GDR. In what follows, I take a closer look at these political dimensions.

My research draws on a broad range of sources. Aside from academic works, reflections, and articles in the specialized and daily press, TV and sound recordings, Internet resources, emails, personal interviews, and conversations with contemporary eyewitnesses, my account is mainly underpinned by archival documents, whether publicly accessible or privately held. A

Figure 1.1 *Silly, 1984, photo session for the album* Zwischen unbefahrenen Gleisen. *From left: Ritchie Barton, Thomas Fritzsching, Tamara Danz, Mathias Schramm, and Herbert Junck © Ute Mahler.*

considerable part of that archival material has remained in the dark until now, and here it is presented for the first time. I hope to acquaint the reader more closely with *Februar* as an artistic milestone, while also using the album as a lens that captures the course of history.

2 Pounding Against the Wall

The Power of Sound

In deeming *Februar* "the soundtrack to the *Wende*" (Pilz 2010, 22) or "funerary music for the GDR" (Dieckmann 1996, 26), the press has suggested that Silly in some way contributed to the fall of the Berlin Wall. Journalistic exaggeration pure and simple, or is there a flicker of truth in the assertion? Music's impact on society has been a source of speculation and debate from time immemorial. In the Bible, trumpets bring down the walls of Jericho; in Plato's *Republic*, Socrates warns of the subversive power of sound, advising that "caution must be taken in adopting an unfamiliar type of music: it is an extremely risky venture, since any change in the musical modes affects the most important laws of a community" (Plato 2008, 128). The opposing camp is no less vocal, with artists themselves often denying any revolutionary influence to music. It's just another commodity for entertainment or introspection, they argue. "It's only rock 'n' roll."

Determining whether rock music was somehow involved in the upheavals of 1989 is anything but straightforward. Asking the question is to venture out on unsteady ground, an ideological minefield as it were. Music's impact can't be measured in mathematical or linear terms; it can only be evaluated discursively. This makes things interesting, but it also makes them challenging.

The means of negotiation are riddled with hegemonic interests, efforts to impose and differentiate one's own reading. The battle lines emerge in keeping with the degree of emotional investment. An outsider might find early swing to be decadent "jungle music," for example, or make out the decline of Western civilization in Elvis Presley's lascivious hip-swings, while the insider rests assured that music is a sublime, transcendent force that makes nobler people of us all, and the world a better place. It would never occur to an insider to connect Rammstein with the massacre at Columbine High School, just as Helene Bøksle fans don't see how the Norwegian mass-murderer Anders Behring Breivik's admiration of the Wagnerian pop singer could hold any relevance to his crime. It doesn't square with their high opinion of Bøksle's music. For them, there isn't any room for destruction.

The extent to which rock music does in fact stir us to action remains indeterminate, or at least difficult to ascertain. In my own argumentation, I follow a discursive line in research on pop music that originates in the field of cultural studies and privileges the link between music and society. In doing so, it views cultural use as essential. Music only acquires meaning through appropriation; otherwise, it is just sound and fury, an acoustic signal. Nor is it a one-way street; music isn't merely set by social and political factors but reflects back on them. Under socialist conditions, the implications for self-empowerment acquired a particular force and gravity.

State and Rock

As with its overall relationship to rock music, the East German state's interventions in the genre sprang fully formed, ideologically speaking, from the dictates of "art as weapon." In the 1960s, a negative view presided that attacked rock music as an insidious means of enemy diversion, with Cold War forces hostile to East Germany's classless society—the reviled *Klassenfeind*—allegedly deploying it to turn youth off the path of socialism. In the early 1970s the tune shifted, with rock music now recognized as a politically expedient tool for propping up state interests (see Rauhut 2002 for greater detail). In due course, the state funded popular music at high cost while also subjecting it to government regulation, erecting a broad scaffold of institutions and laws, and monopolizing the production and release of rock and pop. A towering security apparatus kept watch over the musical landscape, while the press, radio, and TV were all brought to heel and public opinion came under censorship. Rock music was charged with helping to fashion the "socialist personality," itself the "foundational goal" of all society's efforts. The "socialist personality" was defined as an ideal being "possessing a comprehensive political, technical, and general scientific knowledge; a class perspective formed by the Marxist-Leninist worldview; set apart by superior intellectual, physical, and moral qualities; imbued with the spirit of collective thought and action; and consciously and creatively working toward the development of Socialism" (Ebert 1975, 249). Measured against the educational aspirations of East German cultural policy, there was never a point at which rock music was apolitical, whether as an artistic achievement or in its role among youth.

Yet the ideological aims that state propaganda trumpeted as underpinning its support of rock music ran counter to the way things actually worked. Rock music is a highly potent force of socialization, serving as a means by which individual people are able to experience society at large. From the outset, its integration into East German cultural policy bore tremendous potential for conflict. The infractions inevitably committed by musicians and fans alike were interpreted by the state as attacks on the system, with the genre taking on an increasingly political character according to the principle of "for every action an equal and opposite reaction." The perpetual mistrust and hypersensitivity of the censors and security services imbued music—and cultural activities associated with it—with a symbolic power that they didn't have elsewhere. In the end, the tight-spun web of regulations intended to secure influence and control had the opposite effect, awakening a creative drive for the forbidden, and spurring on the hunt for loopholes or blind spots in the system.

In retrospect, this line of development has prompted impassioned debate as to whether rock was merely tolerated as a pressure release valve that provided cover for the prevailing conditions, or did in fact exert a subversive influence. Polish musicologist Jolanta Pekacz argues that the state did succeed in domesticating "rebellious" sounds and rhythms, and that rock music and socialism never stood opposed to one another: "Relationships between the socialist state and rock were more often symbiotic than contradictory, hence many rock musicians were more interested in 'adapting' to the *status quo*, rather than in destroying it"; the "rock 'revolt' was not *against* the dominant culture, but *within* it. The breakup of the Communist bloc was caused by inherent structural contradictions, rather than by a process of 'democratization' forced from below, and even less by attempts to 'repair' a malfunctioning real socialism" (Pekacz 1994, 48).

Peter Wicke, the elder statesman of German pop research, sees it differently. He contends that musicians helped set the stage for the tumult of 1989 by gradually sharpening political consciousness within the general population. In the GDR, rock music brought a liberating sense of connection to the rest of the world, a feeling that counteracted the "uniform gray of socialist reality" (Wicke 1996, 11) and evolved into specific identity markers and patterns of communication. Over the long term, the effects were considerable:

> Music is a medium which is able to convey meaning and values which—even (or, perhaps, particularly) when concealed within the indecipherable world of sound—can shape patterns of behavior imperceptibly over time until they become the visible background of real political activity. In this way, rock music contributed to the erosion of totalitarian regimes throughout Eastern Europe long before the cracks in the system became apparent and resulted in its unexpected demise. (Wicke 1992, 81)

It wasn't the emancipatory efforts of musicians and fans on their own that undermined and eroded the political directives, but dynamics that resided within the state apparatus itself, like a genetic defect. State machinery hardly operated in as monolithic or standardized a fashion as the slogans suggested. The administration suffered from conflicts of interest and "indescribable incompetence" (Wicke 1996,

14); the principle of expediency frequently prevailed, and the chosen path was often the one of least resistance. Nor were the front lines rigidly defined; if a deciding functionary chose to take a risk, critical rock music would make it into the media, or an anarchist band might take the stage at a state-run youth club.

A second essential dynamic that disrupted what was supposedly a "closed trade" was a "terrifying degree of arbitrariness" (ibid.). Laws and statutes were enforced unevenly, at times bent or ignored. Internally, the legal gray zone in which musicians moved was well-known, yet that knowledge was applied on an individual basis and with strategic discretion. Artists who had fallen from favor found themselves sidelined by a customs violation or tax problems; you turned a blind eye for others. Nor did artistic censorship follow a uniform scheme. There was zero tolerance for lyrics that were openly critical of the GDR, but personal and institutional interests left room for finer distinctions. In this way, any number of songs that retain their rebellious potential even today made it through the filters.

The contradictions and tensions that governed the relationship between the East German state and rock music in turn provided an important source of torque; the constant friction cost both energy and illusions, but also spurred on creativity. Musicians found room to maneuver in between the gaps, steadily softening the ground and ultimately undermining the system. Below I explore three areas where this was the case, each of which played an important role in Silly's history as a band.

Enclaves of Self-Empowerment

Relations of Production

The break with political principles was most visible in the realm of music production. Under Marxist-Leninist doctrine, socialism was founded on "society's ownership over the means of production"; private property was considered the root of exploitation and oppression, and thus reactionary. By definition industrial plants and agricultural estates in the GDR belonged to the people, administered under the Socialist Unity Party of Germany (the Sozialistische Einheitspartei Deutschland, SED), which served as the "conscious and organized vanguard of the working class" (Böhme 1988, 878). It fell to the party to ensure stability and growth by structuring the economy according to the "principles of management and planning" (Verfassung 1984, 9).

Artistic production similarly lay within the purview of the state, which ran the studios, publishing houses, media, and distribution channels. It also controlled musicians' training and public performances. State administrations were hierarchical and broken into numerous small departments, each answering to a different authority that ran according to fixed rules. While rock music was conceived in analogy to the state-run economy, in terms of "socialist relations of production" (Wicke 1987, 181), its development was unthinkable without private initiative. As a global art form, rock music operated under premises and norms dictated by the entertainment industry in the West. Ultimately, the only acts that mattered to GDR audiences took their sonic and visual cues from international trends—a dynamic that stood diametrically opposed to state structures set on "independence" and "separation" from "class enemies." Then came the restrictions imposed by the shortage economy, the unending scarcity of resources under socialism. Given the circumstances, small-scale capitalist relationships quietly took root.

Professional rock bands operated de facto as independent businesses. The average value of their technical equipment ran anywhere from 200,000 to 750,000 East German marks, astronomical figures by GDR standards. A majority of the instruments and PAs came from the West. The domestic range of goods plainly failed to meet quality standards, which meant that just about every last rock musician in the GDR was heavily involved in the black market, and constantly flouting foreign currency and customs regulations.

Still, it was in the field of music production that the state principle of centralized management and planning was most seriously compromised. With the capacities of state broadcasting and the state record label far from sufficient and their technical equipment scarcely able to keep pace with developments abroad, wealthy musicians seized the initiative and built out their own private studios—around thirty over the course of the 1980s. More than half worked closely with the media. Through the end of the decade, these studios were responsible for the better part of the rock music produced in the GDR, delivering 80 percent of new releases for broadcast and vinyl pressing in 1988, while further supplying the underground with self-distributed cassettes. Parallel economic structures thus successively established themselves, breaking up the monopoly of the state in the process.

Silly did not have a studio of their own in the GDR but aimed straight for an international stage. After licensing their 1986 record *Bataillon d'Amour* to CBS, Silly released *Februar* as a coproduction between Amiga, the East German state's label, and BMG Ariola, headquartered in Munich. The LP was recorded and mixed in West Berlin in fall 1988, then released in West and East. For the band, the Wall came down a year before the GDR itself collapsed.

A Pact with Fans

At home, Silly's international profile drew a large following taken in by the aura of the West, which long stood as the gold standard in the GDR. Western trends and fashion seeped in, but so too did the ideological fixed points of youth culture centered around music, images, and attitudes that were promptly translated into the terms of everyday life in the GDR and invested with new meaning. For its followers, rock music came to offer a counterproposal to the state's paternalistic aspirations for educating its citizens and cookie-cutter vision of humanity. Instead, rock nurtured identities that strove for emancipation and individuality, opening up alternative contexts and means of communication. The settings and pockets of action that established themselves under the auspices of rock allowed for experiences otherwise forbidden by officialdom to pool, places to live out one's proclivities in the real world. Out on the dance floor or at a show, it became possible to commune with like-minded people and to celebrate being different, to feel free for a couple of hours.

Beyond whatever aesthetic reservations the latest musical styles were forever provoking, it was primarily rock's social impact that set off alarm bells within the halls of power. The state viewed teenagers striking out on their own, off the prescribed pathways as a frontal assault on its mandate; there was real danger here of its actual aim—realizing the ideal "socialist personality" nationwide—slipping from grasp. It reacted accordingly, with the Ministry for State Security (Ministerium für Staatssicherheit, MfS), or Stasi, adopting a particularly harsh stance. From the mid-1960s onward, as Beatlemania swept the GDR along into a new cultural era, the Stasi systematically infiltrated the rock music scene, eliminating ringleaders and trying to regain lost ground. State security recruited countless informers who left no rock unturned in gathering information and making their influence felt. "Unofficial collaborators" (Inoffizielle Mitarbeiter, IM), as they were called, held administrative positions in state institutions and the media, working as managers, technicians, writers, and composers. The "inner circle" of the rock music scene came under special scrutiny as a pit of smoldering "security issues." By 1966 the ministry had decreed that "constant operational control must be ensured through targeted recruiting among members of western-oriented music groups and their followers" (MfS 1966, 43), a strategy it would maintain to the last.

Silly made a repeated point about the symbiotic "pact" they had with fans. As singer Tamara Danz explained, "our common cause ultimately made us what we are, and in a way we have their protection. In turn we're really obliged to stand up for their interests and problems" (Danz 1990, 17). The first Silly fan club was formed in early 1982 by a fourteen-year-old in East Berlin, who found around forty like-minded souls throughout East Germany. Sometimes the club helped the musicians in sending out autographs, but mostly went to concerts together and regularly mobilized votes for the band on the GDR hit parade.

Studies conducted at Humboldt University's Center for Popular Music Research in Berlin speak to the foundational role the band played in fans' forming their identities. The research drew on upward of 13,000 letters received by Silly's management within a year of *Mont Klamott*'s release in 1983. Nearly all included requests for an autograph, a sticker, buttons, or a poster. More detailed analysis of a representative sample—740 letters from May 1984—showed that 43 percent also contained clear-cut value judgments about the band's music, lyrics, and image, or even sought dialogue with the artists. The vast majority of senders were just entering their teenage years; though still quite young, they left no doubt about the tremendous importance that Silly had in their lives. "You're the only ones in the GDR people can actually take seriously," wrote one (Erber 1988, 249). "At least your songs have some kind of meaning, it isn't just slick garbage" (Voos 1985, 54). One seventeen-year-old wrote to Tamara Danz "seeking comfort." Suffering within the dreary confines of the East German countryside, he professed that "I escape from this coldness with your awesome music" (ibid., appendix). Many fans wrote about their everyday lives, "their relationship to the people around them, work, friends, conflicts," hoping for an encouraging word (ibid., 60). They saw both things in the band: stars, and partners in crime.

Fraught Freight

While Silly's output functioned as a multifaceted, all-around work of art, the band's lyrics stood out as a trademark, possessing rare poetry and depth. As a rule, what rock bands sang in their songs held special importance in the GDR—for fans and the state alike. For the powers that be, song lyrics carried a political mission of helping to educate the "socialist personality," and thus stabilize the system. Rock music, in one example of state jargon, was "well-suited to promulgating the attractions of living in peace and under socialism, strengthening the will to live, demonstrating pride in what has been accomplished, and fostering civic attitudes and activities, while also revealing contradictions and engaging in the struggles of our time with the means at its disposal" (Generaldirektion 1984).

Two institutions produced music in the GDR: The Rundfunk, or state broadcasting, and VEB Deutsche Schallplatten, a state-owned enterprise (Volkseigener Betrieb, VEB) whose label Amiga oversaw the field of popular music.

The law gave the two a clear monopoly, banning private companies or other forms of competition. One of the basic requirements for artists to work in the state-run studios was that they express themselves in their mother tongue. Given the strident form of "independence" that ideological dictates demanded, rock musicians in the East were singing in German years before it became popular to do so in West Germany. In a certain respect, the commandants of cultural policy scored a self-goal with the decree. For even as dogged debates over the habitual characteristics or musical omnipotence of the West flagged in time—whether about hair length or "hot

Figure 2.1 *Amiga Studio in East Berlin, 1983, during production of* Mont Klamott. *From left: Thomas Fritzsching, Tamara Danz, sound engineer Helmar Federowski, and Mathias Schramm © Ulrich Burchert.*

rhythms"—it proved impossible to shake the specters that had been summoned with regard to lyrics. They were an object of dispute up to the bitter end, the thing that tipped the scales when it came to decisions about whether something was worthy of production or broadcast.

State broadcasting, the Rundfunk answered directly to the agitation department of the SED's Central Committee, and was thus bound by strict lines of argumentation, with little room for deviation. In its "Lektorat," the broadcaster had a censorship body composed of specialists and cultural functionaries that monitored compliance with the party line, convening once a week to discuss new productions. Music was of secondary concern at the meetings, which revolved almost exclusively around song lyrics. The "basic criteria for acceptance of a title" was defined as its "unity of subjectivity, originality, and partisanship," with "linguistic beauty, safety, and accuracy" serving as further points of reference (Rundfunk 1976). Anything that failed to satisfy the woolly attributes and was deemed either sensitive or aesthetically unappealing was left by the wayside.

VEB Deutsche Schallplatten was subordinate to the Ministry of Culture and enjoyed somewhat greater leeway in its decisions. While it had its political marching orders, there were also economic interests to weigh, which brought a greater willingness to take risks. "I ran the company like a commercial enterprise, not an ideological one," head of Amiga René Büttner put it neatly. Ultimately, the label had a business plan to accomplish: "I had to turn a profit of 3.5 million marks annually. That meant at least 100 million marks in revenue" (Osang 1997, 62). Economic pressures subverted the principle of total affirmation, every now and then allowing critical songs past as an incentive to buy.

The varying degrees of independence between Amiga and the Rundfunk led to paradoxical results. More controversial titles from Amiga often wound up on state broadcasting's no-fly list, as happened to Silly on multiple occasions when authorities caught a whiff of heresy or implicit social critique in their songs. The lyrics voiced truths that went missing from the newspaper or fully contradicted the state's mindless triumphalism, telling of gnawing doubts or dismal fates; the trials and tribulations of the daily rounds; unsatisfied longings or disillusion, resistance and self-assertion; or state environmental crimes. This fraught freight, wrapped up in eloquent images and delivered in between the lines, gave fans a sense of hope and fostered community among those who weren't swimming with the current. In the end, it was the source of a number of "cracks in the system" that brought even walls to topple.

3 The Story of the Band

Familie Silly

Silly's trajectory may come as a surprise to those with a black-and-white image of the GDR. Though atypical, scarcely believable at times, it reveals a great deal about the true nature of East Germany's complex social and political landscape. Contrary to what state propaganda and the incontrovertible existence of the Wall might have suggested, the system in the East wasn't airtight. Niches, pockets of freedom, subtle opportunities for self-realization existed. The principle of authoritarian control was hardly absolute in practice, curbed by the "human factor," whether in the form of empathy or the lower instincts. Individual party functionaries didn't necessarily stand blindly or ideologically opposed to free art, or rule with an iron fist; more often they were opportunists bent on personal advantage, keeping their sails trimmed to the prevailing political winds, and any sympathies concealed behind a show of loyalty to the party line. In some cases, functionaries were even fans who didn't out themselves as such. It is these shades of gray, these contradictions and opportunities to which Silly's story bears witness, culminating in *Februar*. The album was the logical outcome of a hard-nosed campaign for artistic freedom, the peak after a winding path. Below I trace the most important stops along the way.

Of the groups present in GDR media, Silly was in a league of their own, set apart by their musical talent, Western styling, and vigilant political gaze. They projected an air of reflection and honesty; they were intellectual and sensual, nonconformist, masters of their own fate—they were stars, yet remained approachable. They were cosmopolitan and unfettered in sound and look, transcending the circumscribed realities of life in East Germany. Any traces of provincialism or stuffiness were lost on them; you could feel they were in search of something.

The generally agreed-upon date for the band's founding is May 28, 1978, the date of their first show, though the core group of Tamara Danz (voc), Thomas Fritzsching (g, voc, comp, ld), and Mathias Schramm (bg, voc, comp, arr) had been active since the spring of 1977 as a dance combo in bars, backed by other musicians. The band covered hits from abroad, performing tunes by The Beatles, Bee Gees, Mother's Finest, or Bob Marley. In summer 1977, the GDR's artist agency arranged a three-month residency for the group at a restaurant on Romania's Black Sea coast. The group returned to Romania for the following two holiday seasons, playing their first arena shows there in 1979, at venues with a 6,000-person capacity. The musicians took advantage of the long spells abroad to work on original repertoire, setting German lyrics from various authors to music that merged reggae, funk, ska, and disco. By April 1979 the band was ready for its close-up, and recorded three songs in the studios of state broadcasting.

By that point Silly had grown to six, with Danz, Fritzsching, and Schramm joined by Ulrich Mann, Manfred Kusno (keyb, voc) and Michael Schafmeier (dr, voc). Officially the band went by Familie Silly [The Silly Family], an unusual turn of phrase that was the product of a compromise. Band leader Thomas Fritzsching initially landed on Silly as a catchy name with an international ring to it that would be colorful enough to spark different associations. His explanation to authorities was that it was the name of Tamara Danz's cat, the band mascot, though it was a ruse. Cultural officials took exception to the anglicism and denied the group's application; it was only the addition of "Familie," with its sweet overtones of collectivism, that won them over. The band members knew from the outset that they would drop the awkward, stuffy sounding name as quickly as possible, and after 1982 went simply by Silly. Even so, the notion of a family that allowed for individuality while sticking together remained the operating principle. The band shared copyrights and royalties just as they did the debt owed for their expensive musical equipment, forming a tight-knit unit offstage as well. There was strength and protection in community that let band members weather even the bad times. They were constantly "pulling each other up," Tamara Danz explained in retrospect. Without the others she might have given up at some point—"on your own, your skin just isn't quite as thick." (Heinze 1990, 11).

Silly's "thick skin," their iron will to self-determination, opened unexpected doors when paired with savvy and a willingness to take risks. This became apparent early on, when the band accomplished a feat no other East German rock act had: Still unable to put out a record in the GDR, Silly released its debut album in West Germany. In the course of their early performances in Romania, Silly had met a West German who connected them to Hansa Records in West Berlin. Hansa took an interest in the aspiring young group and turned to GDR state broadcasting for material to put out a record. Unwilling to let an opportunity for hard currency slip by, Rundfunk officials agreed to a deal, and Silly was given permission to record at the studios of GDR Broadcasting in May and June of 1980, under exclusive conditions. Eight songs found their way onto the Hansa LP, which appeared four months later across Western Europe. Collaborations of this sort—sleeping with the *Klassenfeind*, so to speak—effectively put a hole in the Wall, and were practically unheard of. At the time the state forbade Silly from traveling to the West, though the band now had an international audience, even without a physical presence.

Behind the scenes, debate raged. In entering unilateral negotiations, the Rundfunk had overstepped its bounds, since the "state monopoly on foreign trade for assigning publishing rights to record companies in the exterior" lay with VEB Deutsche Schallplatten. The state broadcaster had also failed to negotiate "influence over the design of the record sleeve," as well as the advertising copy (Czerny 1980). Patience wore thinner still when the band threw a private record release party in the Pankow district of East Berlin and invited label representatives from Hansa. The escapade had fateful consequences for Silly. The people's own Amiga label, which had previously declined to work more closely with the band, now felt pressure to act and came out with a Silly record of its own one year after the West. *Tanzt keiner Boogie?* [Doesn't Anybody Boogie?] featured nine tracks, six of which also appeared on the Hansa album.

Breakthrough

With its 1983 follow-up, *Mont Klamott*, Silly's image changed as the band broke through onto the East German rock scene. Until *Mont Klamott*, Silly had been filed away under pop, or Schlager music. When it carried 1981's Grand Prix "Golden Lyre" at "Bratislavska Lyra," an international festival of popular music held in Bratislava, the gates of the GDR media swung open. The band switched from GDR Broadcasting to Amiga and entered the premiere league of established acts. *Mont Klamott* exploded when Amiga released it. The album represented a quantum leap where its artistry was concerned, beyond comparison with any other GDR production. The sound was pithy, subtle, and modern, with the bite of new wave. The lyrics wed poetry with disquiet, transmitting messages seldom heard in public. The contrast to the increasingly colorless output from the bloated professional class of rockers couldn't have been greater.

Silly was releasing their material at the right time. *Mont Klamott* became possible in the wake of a cultural policy shift that the SED announced in 1982, in conjunction with the media, the Ministry of Culture, and the Free German Youth (Freie Deutsche Jugend, FDJ). It wasn't lost on GDR authorities that rock music in East Germany was rife with lethargy and losing its value. Summarizing a trend in the genre toward "non-committal textual content" and a "loss of substance," one internal analysis from the cultural department of the SED Central Committee called for greater openness to international influence. Unorthodox trends like punk or new wave should continue to receive scrutiny, but no longer be rejected out of hand. The goal instead should be to harness music's positive potential, its "fresh and light-hearted" qualities, theatrical aspects, or "elements of humor, satire, and even nonsense," though "socially concrete" song lyrics and their "representation of day-to-day issues and real-life situations" retained pride of place. The document argued for greater "courage and trust," warning against "looking to prevent something with bans" (all citations: ZK der SED 1982).

This meant Silly's ambition of playing topical, professional rock music that reached for deeper meaning unfurled with the winds of cultural policy at its back. For many fans, as for the arts section in the papers, the main attraction proved to be the moral and intellectual position that revealed itself through the band's lyrics. From *Mont Klamott* on, Silly worked exclusively with lyricist Werner Karma, whose words became a hallmark of the band. Karma was an extraordinary poetic talent, capable of vivacious, sensual, highly refined images that scoured the depths of human experience and spoke to the times directly from the heart. In Karma's lines, listeners found coded messages about daily life on the terms of "real socialism." Subtly but unerringly, the words unearthed taboos, managing simultaneously as pure poetry and plain speech. Through his lyrics, Karma looked to give voice to the "doubting, unruly spirit" (Karma 2023, interview).

In Tamara Danz, Werner Karma found a kindred spirit to interpret his work. "From the very beginning quite an uncommon intimacy" existed between the two (Karma 2021, 62), which the songwriter also described as a "creative liaison that would endure for seven years." The "deal" was simple: "You give everything, and get nothing less in return" (Karma 2002,

308). For her part, Danz took Karma to be a genius, seeing herself reflected in his emotions and positions and explaining that "I would write lyrics in exactly the same way if I could, so I sing them like they were my own" (Jacobus 1987, 7). Karma never wrote from a distance but used the first person, reflecting the large in the small. Poet and singer alike saw an unapologetic first-person perspective as a condition for reaching others.

As a student of philosophy, Werner Karma had cut his teeth writing songs for musical theater. Preferring to cast a blind eye to his avowed affinity for the GDR, censors labeled him "fame-hungry" and "in need of counsel" (Steineckert 1984a). Karma had one piece after another banned by the Rundfunk; the broadcaster's censorship body accused him of distorting reality with "excessive subjectivism" and "taking flight into the illusionary as opposed to the present moment." His implicit "protest" was "undialectical and absolutizing," setting things in "skewed proportions" (Rundfunk 1982). Some texts had to be submitted up to seven times over, subject to endless revisions. Functionaries were obviously just as capable of reading between the lines as the public. Yet with any political discontent masked in lyrical form and never conceded by the creators, debate stayed on the surface, with each side speaking past the other. "The attacks on the lyrics often had something helpless and comical about them," Karma later recalled (Karma 2002, 316).

The Rundfunk didn't simply force changes to a number of Silly's early songs but banned multiple songs produced by Amiga from broadcast, including "Dicke Luft" [Thick Air] and "Die Gräfin" [The Countess]. The latter had originally been brought to state broadcasting for recording but ran up against the censors' veto. The song tells the story of an elderly woman living on the fringes of society, consigned to oblivion and awash in gloom, without hope of happiness. She drowns her loneliness in "Korn and Kümmel," dwelling on better times that likely never were. Fates like hers didn't match the triumphant tone of SED propaganda and otherwise went missing from the public eye. In depicting "the countess" as a neighbor, Silly restored her dignity; in the final verse, Tamara Danz sings, "one floor down from me there lives an old woman / she's faded and gray as our block / Whenever I think I'm tired I just think of her / and die laughing at my own lot." "Cynical and disparaging! Title rejected!" read the censors' verdict (Rundfunk 1981). Silly took the song along with other redacted material to Amiga, where it found someone willing to listen. Editor-in-chief René Büttner gave the heretical songs a pass for *Mont Klamott* and continued to stand up for the band in the years to come. Karma credited Büttner's solid "backbone," speculating that "without him all our power would probably have come to nothing" (Karma 1997, 220).

Changing over from the Rundfunk to Amiga brought Silly considerably more artistic freedom. René Büttner made the band a top priority, personally supervising each release and ordering changes only when risky subjects, images, or buzzwords threatened to derail the overall product. Tactical considerations led Büttner to strike "Dicke Luft" from the final track list for *Mont Klamott* completely. In alluding to the GDR's environmental crimes, the song flirted with a forbidden topic. A city suffocates beneath unbearable air pollution, the firmament darkens like a "black ribbon," turning day into night. Disaster looms: "Sometimes I dream that a war / between us and the sky is in store / We shoot up / the sky shoots back /

Figure 3.1 *Press Conference for* Mont Klamott, *1983. From left: Werner Karma, Tamara Danz, René Büttner, Thomas Fritzsching © Ulrich Burchert.*

And neither one / has backed down yet." Though Büttner didn't allow "Dicke Luft" on the album, he did release it as a single. His instincts hadn't deceived him; the song was banned from East German media nationwide. It didn't stop the band from playing it regularly at shows.

Adapting and Resisting

Mont Klamott set off a run of success for the band that would continue unabated. Silly records sold exceedingly well in the

GDR, nearly a million copies in total, with every last one polling as "LP of the year" among East German critics. The band took up permanent residence on the hit parade and became the darling of the arts section, while frontwoman Tamara Danz was hailed as "Rock Lady," repeatedly voted "singer of the year" by the trade press and fans alike. Step by step, Danz and her band joined the ranks of the cultural establishment. The Committee for Entertainment Arts, a special panel within the Ministry of Culture, took the band under its wing, providing funding and logistical support. In 1986, Tamara Danz met GDR head Erich Honecker at a reception for the East German Peace Council, and in 1987, the band received the GDR's art award. Silly performed at the "Festival of Political Song" and the Free German Youth's large-scale "Rock for Peace" event and was sent abroad to allied socialist countries as a cultural export.

Critics have accused the band of conforming and serving as a sort of handmaiden to the system. But was that really the case? Any rock musician who climbs onstage or enters the studio does so in the hopes of generating as large an audience as possible, no matter where or under what societal conditions. Everyone wants to be heard. Questions of principle confront those who would court success: Do I play by the rules of the game, or steer clear of them? Do I enter the cycles of media and industry, or carve out a niche in the underground? Do I bow to the dictates of money and politics, or follow my own lead? What price am I willing to pay? The majority of musicians in the GDR opted to come to terms with power; they varied in how far they went. Silly took the institutional path, though without letting themselves be coopted. They remained alert and nonconformist, managing to strike a clever balance and identify allies within the state apparatus. Holding socialism as the better model, they chose critical engagement over retreat. The band supported the state-led peace movement and took an active role in cultural policy arguments regarding rock music's place in East Germany, and issues with its development. In the end phase of the GDR, they strove for a reformed version of socialism, staying true to their principles even after 1989.

In the political and social turmoil surrounding 1989, the *Wende* as it is known in German, many zeroed in on Tamara Danz as the "Voice of the East" in her efforts to find a third way, a political alternative between the opposite poles of socialism and capitalism that would uphold justice and maintain values worth defending. On talk shows and interviews but also through song, Danz took aim at the retroactive leveling of experience in the GDR, the wholesale dismissal of her country and the crowing of the victors. In their place, she advocated reason and a sense of proportion. Shortly after the Wall came down, at the height of political reckoning with the "Honecker Regime," she noted with a view to her profession that "things were substantially more pluralistic than is talked about in retrospect. Today everything is lumped together as if it was all shit" (Danz 1990, interview).

After 1989, critics of East Germany charged Danz and her colleagues with looking back at the system through glasses colored rosy by privilege. In fact, the musicians were drawing on a much broader array of experiences than the average citizen. After finally receiving permission to travel in the mid-1980s, Silly had gotten to know the West and been introduced to other forms of power and censorship. As a band that continued to see its place as being in the GDR, the experience put things at home into perspective. The musicians in Silly were also able to explore and develop themselves to a much greater extent than was possible for most people. Shielded by their tremendous popularity, they weren't forced to hide their individuality away in private, but were able to put it on full public display. The band freed itself from the egalitarian pressures of the GDR.

The moral doubters often measured Silly one-sidedly by the way things looked on the surface, their fame and popularity in the media, thereby disregarding the struggles that continued behind the scenes. While conflicts between the band and the state were perennial, they took on a different quality in the second half of the 1980s as the band sought more radical measures to elude the government's grip. Long since financially independent and celebrated in the West, their autonomy increased to a point where they were considered "no longer manageable" internally (MfS 1987). In 1987, Silly declined to make an appearance at the prestigious "Rock for Peace" event, feeling that they were being instrumentalized. Tamara Danz didn't shy away from piling scorn on the Stasi at shows, settling accounts with the media, or demanding freedom to travel abroad. Everything was noted down in scrupulous detail.

In September of 1987, the Ministry of Culture issued a comprehensive report on the "Development of the Group Silly." Classified "strictly confidential," the ten-page document serves as a remarkable snapshot of the era, setting the political erosion of those years into sharp focus, the "new thinking" of the Gorbachev era that ultimately allowed an album like *Februar* to be released in the first place. In a sign of its politically explosive nature, the secret report was forwarded to the Politburo of the Central Committee, the locus of power within the SED. The Ministry of Culture sketched the course of things to date, inquiring into the root causes and drawing "conclusions for international work in the field of the entertainment arts." Silly was described as the country's "highest profile and most creative band at present," and Tamara Danz as a "highly-talented artist, an interesting voice and fascinating personality." Granting Silly permission to perform in the West had brought "growing issues in dealing with the group." Overall communication had become more difficult, with Tamara Danz's behavior especially sending "alarming signals." She refused to show the state the requisite appreciation and took a "demonstratively naive outlook on the political assessment of artistic activity." SED functionaries observed uneasily that the band "pursued a highly commercial concept, striking an increasing distance from the GDR on that basis."

The search for reasons to explain the blatant loss of control yielded an astonishing degree of governmental self-critique. The strategy document cited a stultifying bureaucracy and petty institutional infighting in the same breath as difficulties within the music business, the scarcity of resources, and financial risk involved in "obtaining technical equipment, replacement parts, and transportation on individual initiative." Compared to the gloomy description of the status quo in its introduction, the paper performed a surprising volte-face in its summary, seeming to cast ironclad principles aside and reading like ideological capitulation. Far from looking to curb the band's westward expansion, the paper advocated vouchsafing "further opportunities for this potent and impactful group to develop." In conjunction with CBS Group, which had signaled interest in the band, it proposed coming up with a plan for Silly's "worldwide engagement."

The document also looked beyond the case at hand, raising "questions of principle" in the field of the "entertainment arts" that demanded "decisions." It assigned top priority to the "commercial marketing" of East German products in the West, to which end travel should be made easier, and "newness" no longer "looked on with deep mistrust," or viewed as hostile to socialism. In the end, it was about standing up to the *Klassenfeind*, who had to be beaten at his own game by his own means, that is "brutal commercialism" (all citations: Ministerium 1987). Within this context, Silly's Western leanings seem less like a frosty farewell to the system than a symptom of serious structural issues that introduced chaos and an arbitrary quality to the state administration of rock music.

Alpha Singer Tamara Danz

The same year that the Ministry for Culture took up the band's cause, praising Tamara Danz as a figure of unique artistic authority, the Stasi filed a character profile casting the singer in a wholly negative light. The report described her as "volatile" and self-centered; she exerted a harmful influence on her professional environment, lacked any "real skills of appraisal," and refused to "integrate herself into cultural policy." In general, it required "greater and greater effort to convince her of positive things" (MfS 1987). Other band members went unmentioned.

Figure 3.2 *Tamara Danz, 1987, backstage in Bremen, West Germany © Jürgen Sieker.*

Danz wasn't simply the voice and face of Silly. From an endless variety of perspectives, whether that of functionaries, the press, or fans, she was perceived as an alpha figure. Born Tamara Leonore on December 14, 1952, in Thuringia in Central Germany, Danz grew up in sheltered circumstances, the only child of a kindergarten teacher and a mechanical engineer. Her father later switched from engineering to the diplomatic service, representing the GDR as a trade advisor in a succession of countries. When Tamara was two, the family moved to Bulgaria, followed by Romania in 1963. In Bucharest, she attended school at the Soviet embassy, learning to speak fluent Russian. In 1967, she returned to East Berlin.

Her father soon fell out of political favor for failing to toe the party line. Suspected of contact with Western spy organizations, he was ousted from the SED and the GDR state prosecutor opened investigations against him. Witnessing the end of her father's career proved just as formative to Danz's worldview as the rift between reality and propaganda she experienced growing up in the Socialist bloc. At fifteen she drew the attention of the East German secret service for demonstrating against the repressive violence of Warsaw Pact troops during the Prague Spring of 1968. Subsequently considered politically unreliable or dangerous and Western in outlook, she was held in suspicion for her pride, flamboyant nature, and readiness to fight.

As a teenager she dove into the alternative world of rock 'n' roll. She loved the music and attitudes of the Rolling Stones, and fell in with a clique of "bums," *Gammler* in the lingo of the day. The group would post up on street corners or park benches to scandalize parents and the squares, with portable radios cranked to the max. Once while still a minor, Danz was caught in a police raid and interrogated by the Stasi. "From that moment on rock 'n' roll and politics were inseparable for me." She now saw "that you had to find a place in society where you had the greatest degree of freedom with the fewest limitations. So I became a singer" (Danz 1997b, 206).

In fall 1972, a friend talked Danz into joining the Oktoberklub, the FDJ's best-known singing club. She stayed a year, meeting a number of fellow members who later came to hold positions of influence, like Gisela Steineckert (President of the Committee for Entertainment Arts), René Büttner (head of Amiga), and Hartmut König (Culture Secretary on the FDJ Central Council). At difficult junctures later on, these contacts opened a number of doors for Danz and Silly. Her first professional gig—and an important apprenticeship—came as one of three female vocalists in the Horst-Krüger-Band, a ten-piece ensemble she stayed with from 1974 through its dissolution in 1976. She joined Familie Silly the next year, at the same time pursuing a certificate in vocal training that she completed in 1979.

With Silly, a new era opened for Danz. She had found allies who broadened her horizons, burned with passion for a shared cause, and were willing to take risks for it. The next years were awash with activity, creative and full of challenges. They allowed the singer to mature into the figure people still remember today. Those who knew Danz credit her with a high level of intelligence, ambition, and a steady moral compass. She was courageous and uncompromising, combative and headstrong. Werner Karma gave a vivid description of how she fought for every last line: "Tamara perches on her songs like a mother hen, pecking away at the political egg-thieves" (Karma 2002, 317). Even if injuries were unavoidable, there was always a way to avert deeper disaster. Unlike other artists who were either banned from performing or forced out of the country, Silly never faced existential danger. They were spared summary judgment, not least because of Danz's strategic wiles as well as her disarming friendliness and irresistible charm. She avoided open confrontation, smoothing over her more refractory qualities with a smile.

As the lead singer of Silly, Tamara Danz also blossomed into a performer capable of commanding interpretations, a wide cast of characters that ranged from vulnerable and mild to cuttingly cold and aggressive. Danz was at once unapproachable and giving, soft as butter and hard as concrete. She gave her imagination free rein to explore the nuances of her vocal range, which extended from a raw, at times smoky alto to a bell-like soprano. The music press hailed her singular ability to shape-shift, now serious and reflective, now sneering, brawny, vulgar. One reviewer wrote that she "seemed fit to burst with dynamism," her manner of singing reflecting back "the feeling of the era" (Lange 1983, 2). Danz also caused a stir with the myriad types of women she evoked, many of which were otherwise all but impossible to find in GDR rock. On the band's debut album *Tanzt keiner Boogie?* Danz slips into the role of a lusty, emancipated woman who inverts gender cliches with her wantonness and hunger for life, only to reveal herself as easily wounded, melancholic, and full of doubts on the B-Side. *Mont Klamott* likewise featured notes of tender femininity and aspects of longing, with Danz enveloping male characters like a mother on a number of tracks, providing warmth and comfort as the voice of experience and strength. Another, rarely explored category was the loser or outcast, a woman scarred by life. No matter their situation, Danz's characters were never without human worth, and always deserving of sympathy.

To her admirers, Danz came across as "authentic," and thus someone to fully identify with, regardless of the "song personality" (Frith 1998, 212) she adopted. The songs that she made flesh and blood enthralled listeners with their sensitivity to everyday realities and the things that truly mattered in life. To the fans, the songs embodied what was worth fighting for—the truth. When she died in 1996 at just forty-three, Danz ascended from idol to myth, a status she retains to this day.

4 Journey to the West

The Passport Battle

Silly's struggle for independence and veracity shouldn't leave any doubts as to the band's commercial ambitions. The musicians were looking to succeed; they wanted to make money, find the spotlight, and, as went without saying, stand up by comparison to the West. Yet the Iron Curtain wasn't all that easy to traverse; only a handful of GDR bands had been granted the privilege. Whether or not an artist received permission to travel abroad to capitalist countries depended in large part on their market value on the other side, since the East German state collected the lion's share of their fees in coveted hard currency. Ultimately, though, gauging a candidate's "political reliability" (Ministerrat 1982, 9) took top priority, even if the difficulties of doing so in a country where "private" opinion gladly hid behind a "public" version of itself gave free rein to caprice. Often, the left hand didn't know what the right was up to, leaving institutions at cross-purposes. As it was, the Stasi had the final word, which it pronounced behind closed doors.

Silly first visited the West in fall 1979, spending a month in the city of Kristiansand in southern Norway. For four and a half hours a night, six nights a week the band, billed as a "show and dance orchestra," played covers at the Hotel Caledonien discotheque. The "Silly Family," as they were dubbed in the local press, returned to Norway the following year, spending all of November in Lillehammer, albeit under more challenging circumstances. Thomas Fritzsching and bandmates now had to cover the singing, since Tamara Danz had been barred from traveling. The authorities had stalled Danz up to the final minute, a common show of power in the GDR, keeping the reasons for the final decision shrouded in silence. The band responded to the authoritarian power play with stubborn resistance, prompting a years-long tug of war that was witness to intrigue and strife, but also the tenacious will of the musicians.

On April 29, 1981, Silly drafted a six-page letter. The band summarized its career to date, professed its political loyalty, and concluded by asking about the reasons for the sudden travel ban. A fourth tour offer from West Germany lay on the desk of the GDR artist agency in the meantime, and the band was being systematically put off (Familie Silly 1981). The letter was addressed to Kurt Hager, head of the Cultural Commission on the Politburo of the SED Central Committee, and one of the GDR's most powerful figures. Hager turned the missive over to the Central Committee's cultural department and asked for clarification. The letter thus began its odyssey across the desks of the party machinery and cultural administration, with nobody feeling themselves responsible. Nearly one and a half years passed. The band wrote Kurt Hager again, casting their letter as a "petition" for added emphasis. The "continued existence of our group" was at stake; the meager opportunities and shuttling without alternative "between Rostock and Suhl" would inevitably bring "artistic and creative death" (Familie Silly 1982). The cry for help didn't elicit the echo it had hoped for. The real reasons behind the matter weren't forthcoming, let alone its resolution, and attempts were made instead to placate the musicians with higher concert fees and greater media presence. After two years of back and forth, Kurt Hager instructed colleagues on the Central Committee "to tell F. [Fritzsching, the band leader] that *I* can't do anything, since I don't know the context. The group ought be active *here* and in other socialist countries" (Hager 1983).

It wasn't the SED pulling the strings but the Ministry for State Security, which had barred Tamara Danz from the West "for security reasons" (MfS 1980). The MfS averred that the singer was "unstable in her political ideology to the point of negativity, and voices progressive thoughts only out of a desire to press her advantage, e.g. at the 'Rock for Peace' event. Multiple sources concur in assessing her politically positive attitude toward the GDR to be a sham" (MfS 1984). This made it reasonable to assume "Danz wouldn't represent the GDR in a worthy manner while abroad in non-socialist countries" (MfS 1985). She was further suspected of intent to flee the country. Silly's front woman guessed who was really running the show and turned up unannounced at the Ministry for State Security on April 29, 1981. Two officers politely heard her out, but ultimately denied any jurisdiction over the case. The singer left unawares of just how squarely she was in the crosshairs. A few weeks prior it had been proposed from on high "to review the incriminating evidence about Danz on file so as to reach final clarification for her possible detachment from the group" (MfS 1981). After Danz's visit to Stasi central, Silly sent their first letter to Kurt Hager.

Unofficial Contact between East and West

Though long unable to travel, the band had a retinue of sympathizers and allies on the other side of the Wall. One of the most important was Jim Rakete, a big name as the manager of Nina Hagen, Nena, and Spliff, among others. A colleague had introduced Rakete to *Mont Klamott* one day, music created just a few miles away as the crow flies, but which nobody in the West was interested in. "We had no idea about the scene in East Germany, none of us had ever listened to it. Our roots lay elsewhere. We were would-be Americans" (Rakete 2023, interview). Sliding the cassette into the tape deck, Jim Rakete entered another world.

> I was just blown away by the lyrics and atmosphere, but also by the fact that somebody was risking a kind of pathos that would have been unthinkable for us. I found it very courageous. The musical landscape in West Berlin was totally different at the time. Pop music poked fun at our parents' generation, the lyrics tended to be cynical. And here came Silly with this truly evocative force. Gosh! I thought. This is something else entirely, they're really telling a story. (ibid.)

Rakete traveled to East Berlin to meet the band and wound up connecting them with CBS Schallplatten GmbH, the German subsidiary of the international industry giant. CBS signaled interest in licensing the forthcoming Silly album. As Amiga wrapped production in September 1984 and began to prepare the release, Tamara Danz passed a copy of the final mix to the graphic designer at CBS at a private meeting, along with song lyrics as inspiration for the cover. Yet things went south; customs intercepted the contraband at the border and confiscated it, and what to date had been an unprecedented coup fell apart at the seams. This time Amiga had signed off on all the lyrics and agreed to maintain confidentiality with Silly, looking to present the hard-liners with a fait accompli. For Werner Karma, the motives were clear: "It smelled quite strongly of West German Marks" (Karma 2002, 319). The record was political dynamite, entitled *Zwischen unbefahrenen Gleisen* [Between Untraveled Tracks].

The case ended up with the Committee for Entertainment Arts, where it was sent upstairs. Committee president Gisela Steineckert brought the matter to the Minister of Culture, warning of an "avalanche." Werner Karma's lyrics would "cause grave and new damage to the entire rock scene and entertainment arts overall." The "foreign currency business" must have deprived the bosses at VEB Deutsche Schallplatten of their sanity—"has the instinct for self-destruction overtaken them, like the lemmings?" (all citations: Steineckert 1984a). The embattled comrades at Deutsche Schallplatten didn't back down, but defended their decision. In conversations with the band, the committee similarly ran up "against granite. They smile for us and offer us interpretations a child wouldn't expect to hear." The artists had been the beneficiaries of a great deal of patience, provided with arguments toned down "especially for the less educated and politically less engaged." The musicians and functionaries engaged in the usual bouts of shadow-boxing, "a species of fruitless discussions where one gradually begins to doubt one's own sanity" (all citations: Steineckert 1984b).

In the end, the Ministry of Culture halted the record's release by executive fiat. The cover was rejected, and three songs had to be rewritten entirely—"Tausend Augen" [Thousand Eyes], about ubiquitous surveillance; "Zwischen unbefahr'nen Gleisen" [Between Untravelled Tracks], about the freedom to travel; and "Nur ein Lied" [Just a Song], which addressed moral integrity. "Tausend Augen," initially planned as the opener, hit especially hard. It derided the GDR "as a total surveillance state" (Steineckert 1984a), leveling itself "against the work of security organizations" (MfS 1984). Tamara Danz sang of "a thousand eyes" lurking around every corner, "behind the wallpaper," "at the root of the city." She also addressed the MfS directly: "A thousand eyes inspect my travel papers." The censored album came out in 1985 under the title *Liebeswalzer* [The Waltz of Love]. It is easy to read the ersatz title as a dig, a mock curtsy to a power one would never bend to. There was no mention of the album's difficult birth in the press, of course—reviewers fell over themselves with praise, hailing *Liebeswalzer* as a masterpiece, sharp, experimental, and perfect all at the same time.

Arrival in the West

This time as well, the intention was to block Silly's commercial ventures in the West. In a last-ditch effort, Tamara Danz petitioned for release from GDR citizenship, filing an "application for departure." In truth, Danz never wanted to leave her country but to apply maximum pressure. The game of brinkmanship paid off, and on March 20, 1985, the singer was authorized as a *Reisekader* to travel abroad to non-socialist countries. Two months later, Silly was put to the litmus test and sent as part of an FDJ delegation to the Laulu Festival in Finland, a political music event. The band gave three performances in Helsinki and a dozen interviews; internal assessment made special note of the band's "strict discipline and high-level of engagement," and credited Silly with "a not inconsequential share" in the festival's overall success (Zentralrat der FDJ 1985). The ice had broken.

In the years to come, Silly toured throughout Scandinavia and beyond, passing through Switzerland, Austria, France, and Portugal. Yet the band found the greatest resonance in West Berlin and West Germany, after *Bataillon d'Amour* turned it into a pan-German phenomenon. The album was recorded at Amiga's studio in 1986 and licensed by CBS in the West. Guest producer Micki Meuser assumed responsibility for computer programming and came from the West bearing all manner of hard and software, resulting in a sound that kept up with international standards. The outcome was more streamlined, sailing less against the wind—the band was clearly headed for the musical mainstream. They had arrived in the West. Booking was steady, with the press paying court to Tamara Danz as the "Tina Turner of the East." The title track off the album was a hit, running on more than a dozen West German TV shows. The same song made just a single appearance on GDR TV; the deciding editors had always taken serious exception to the "group's external bearing" and kept their presence to a minimum (ZK der SED 1983).

This type of bottlenecking and chicanery had less and less of an effect as the years went on. By the end of the 1980s, Silly had undeniably broken free of the clutches of the socialist rock administrators, achieving a large degree of autonomy. They nearly gave the impression of being a Western band that lived in the East, no longer forced to submit to an involved application process every time they traveled abroad, but holding long-term visas that also applied for their spouses or life partners. Moving in between two worlds, they found an audience in both. As was common with GDR exports, the band was initially perceived in the West as a sort of exotic species. Musicians from the East were often patronized, treated as creatures seemingly descended from a foreign star, with an overall bearing that was just as homespun and alien as their sound and metaphor-laden lyrics. They were written off as "inhibited" (Karma 2023, interview).

Perceptions varied between East and West, at times running contrary to one another. Fans in the GDR marveled at the band's unmistakably "Western" appeal; to them Silly were cosmopolitan, hip, and innovative, cutting a brilliant contrast to the uniform gray of the daily grind. Western observers, meanwhile, smirked at their clothing, the overblown accessories and tousled hair. Jim Rakete voiced in retrospect what many were thinking at the time:

> Stylistically they had aligned themselves with an era I would describe as akin to Goth. Their hair stood straight up, like they had both hands plugged into a socket. They also looked like they had fallen into a paintbox, truly prodigal amounts of eyeliner had been applied. I just stood there slack-jawed the first time I met them. They looked so dramatic, like the riders of the Apocalypse. (Rakete 2023, interview)

Figure 4.1 *The Palace of the Republic in East Berlin during the "Rock for Peace" festival, January 1987. Awarded "Band of the Year 1986," Bataillon d'Amour was also selected as "Hit of the Year"; the eponymous record was named "LP of the Year" with over 300,000 units sold. Silly accepted the prizes, but didn't make an appearance © Gabriele Senft.*

Silly had appeared intermittently in the West German press before they were allowed to cross the border themselves; in 1985 Zweites Deutsches Fernsehen (ZDF) introduced them to a broad audience with a ten-minute band portrait. Once it was finally possible to see the band live, the media reported regularly on the group from "over there." The tenor of the press was uniformly positive, hailing Silly's worldliness and predicting a brilliant future. The passions that Tamara Danz stirred with her aura of self-assurance and arresting voice made her an especially "ideal candidate for pursuing a career in West Germany" (Schmidtendorf 1986, 29). Denmark's largest daily paper dispensed knightly accolades after the band performed at the rock festival in Skanderborg in August 1987, writing that while

Eastern European bands were always said to lag ten years behind the times, Silly had proved the opposite to be the case. The group had quite simply overshadowed most of the acts at the festival, and were "fifteen years ahead at least" (Lambertsen 1987, 7).

It wasn't Silly's artistic profile alone that held media interest among the *Klassenfeind*, of course, but the political story. Throughout the many interviews they gave, the musicians never shied away from discussing the "critical closeness" they felt toward the GDR (Richter 1988, 141). The band found that people in the GDR showed greater solidarity with one another, while everything on the other side was "somewhat more fleeting and more surface." None of the band members took staying in the West for an option; as Tamara Danz uttered laconically, "I don't find it so nice at all over here" (Leitner 1989). As for fleeing, she viewed it as the "path of least resistance." The end equation was plain to see: "If you can't fight at home, you aren't going to make it in the West either" (Schulz 1987, 40). Asked whether she thought the "Wall would come down at some point," she replied "Yes. At some point, yes." She came out as a supporter of Mikhail Gorbachev, who "really was a ray of hope" in a "dark" time for world politics (all citations: Richter 1988, 141 and 142). One prominent weekly picked up on Danz's admission, photographing the band wearing "Gorbi" buttons in front of the Brandenburger Tor, and titling the piece "Glasnost by the Score" (Lahann 1989).

The Origins of *Februar*

The article headline hit home, even if it had a sensational ring. Just a few weeks before Silly had released *Februar*—their final

GDR record, and one that breathed the new spirit of openness demanded by Gorbachev's reformist politics. *Februar* was both an artistic masterstroke and the band's most incendiary work, with multiple songs broaching the bankruptcy of the system and hope for change. The same sentiment announced itself in the title, "February," the last month in winter preceding the thaw. It wasn't just in terms of content that the record marked the culminating point of rock music's political history in the GDR, but its logistics. As a coproduction between East and West, the album represented an absolute exception in divided Germany, a chance granted no other band. Silly had achieved its long-term goal: they weren't just releasing albums in the West, they were producing them there as well. In the press kit assembled by Ariola, the musicians revealed that they "finally wanted to make a record with as much force as the live show. But to do so we needed a kind of technology and work environment that we couldn't find in the GDR" (BMG Ariola 1989).

Thomas Stein had been the one to set the levers in motion as the head of Ariola at Bertelsmann Music Group (BMG), a global player. Stein added Silly to Ariola's roster, a star-studded lineup primarily made up of Schlager acts, after meeting the band in the GDR. Recognizing Silly's unique status, Stein assigned the project top priority, looking to add extra luster to Ariola's portfolio but also hoping to stake a claim in the East, whose market grew more interesting by the day amid the societal changes. While *Februar* was defined in the contract and on the cover as a joint East-West production, it was Ariola that footed the bill. Stein recalled that "VEB Deutsche Schallplatten didn't really have any more money at the time as it was. It was clear to me from the outset that we would finance everything. Recording took much longer than we originally anticipated, things got much more expensive. But it didn't bother me, since I firmly believed that Silly deserved it" (Stein 2023, interview). The unequal partnership brought a considerable advantage: "I told René Büttner [at Amiga] that if we were going to pay for everything, we were also going to make the decisions. You guys please just nod along in agreement. We would do whatever we thought we could market" (ibid.). Conflict remained inevitable of course, flaring up over the political import of a number of songs. Management at Amiga may have reared its head, but in the end, it bowed to the power of the purse.

Under Amiga's initial plans, *Februar* was actually slated to be recorded in the East and mixed in the West. Silly spent a brief window at Amiga's studio late in the summer of 1988 arranging, recording, and working on rough mixes. Yet worlds lay in between the outcome and the eventual end result; they sounded completely different. Amiga's studio may have had a solid analog set-up, but it hadn't entered the digital age and had no computerized technology to draw on, leaving it unable to keep pace internationally. With Ariola footing the bill and insisting on top quality, in the end the decision was to produce the record entirely in the West. The choice fell on Preußen Tonstudio in Kreuzberg, Berlin, with whose staff the band had long been on friendly terms. Nearly every day over the course of three months in fall 1988, Silly crossed the border out of East Berlin to the other side to record. Uwe Hoffmann, co-owner of the studio and an experienced drummer in his own right, took on the role of producer.

Since their last album, Silly had recruited two new members who left a substantial imprint on the band's overall sound and songwriting and drove them along creatively. Uwe Hassbecker (g, v) and Jäcki Reznicek (bg) were both masters of their instruments. Both looked the part as well, emanating charisma and raising the band's visual appeal. Jim Rakete thought it was this latter aspect that mattered to Danz: "Uwe and Jäcki are marvelous musicians, no doubt. But I still think that Tamara sought them out in part because they looked cool and were so confident on stage. Presence played an important role for her" (Rakete 2023, interview). By this point, Silly's founder Thomas Fritzsching had taken a side role; while the cover still listed him in the lineup, he didn't play a single note on the album.

The record proved a challenge to make, and a learning process for all involved. Thomas Stein, who still calls *Februar* his "dream project" today, spoke about it in terms of a "culture clash."

> Musicians from the GDR were much better trained than many of their counterparts in West Germany. But they used a different language. A lot remained incomprehensible to us. That was what was so remarkable, that people in East and West Germany expressed themselves in totally different ways. The discrepancy led to tension. I was always telling Silly that if they wanted to succeed in the West, people had to be able to understand what they were singing about. No one had any idea what they meant with "there's a specter haunting Mitropa." We had some real blow-outs about some of the lyrics. It was an exhausting process. Tamara & Co. made as if they were considering changes, but it was more for show, so that I would

> leave them in peace. They had grown up in entirely different structures after all, and had gotten by just fine with their own philosophy thus far. And then someone like me comes along and starts criticizing their recipe for success . . . They didn't know how to write a song in German that could also be marketed in the West. It was a long, tough process to come to terms with each other. But that's how it is in the creative world, conflict is unavoidable. Today you don't find any kind of discussion whatsoever. Sadly. (Stein 2023, interview)

With *Februar*, Silly made a quantum leap artistically, while further detaching themselves from GDR cultural policy. The album marked a new chapter in band history for another reason as well: During production they broke with Werner Karma. The first cracks in the relationship had appeared after *Bataillon d'Amour*, as the old idea of the family began to crumble. Marketing had pushed Tamara Danz further and further to the front; her likeness decorated the album cover of *Bataillon d'Amour* in 1986, and the media cast her in the spotlight as the heart and engine of Silly. As Danz grew increasingly self-sure and assertive over the band, hierarchies formed. Mathias Schramm, formerly the band's artistic mastermind and bassist, was replaced with Jäcki Reznicek; Thomas Fritzsching took a backseat to focus on organizational matters. Looking back, Werner Karma saw Tamara Danz blinded by the neon lights coming from the other side:

> Once Tamara was finally allowed to travel and I drove around the West with her meeting musicians and journalists, I observed how she soaked up everything they told her about

> the big, wide world and the music business. I noticed what an impression she let it make on her. She had no immune system, she fell for the hocus-pocus. I was immune. My father fought as a communist resisting the Nazis and went into emigration. After the war he chose the GDR. His path marked my own. The West was never an option for me. But Tamara, it seemed to me, was taken in by consumer society. Unfortunately, she went ahead and tried to make her band just as "pretty." By changing the lineup, and in its appearance. (Karma 2023, interview)

Worldviews drifted still further apart with the new signals coming from Moscow. While Danz made a point of wearing her Gorbachev button, Karma himself was leery of the "heavy wrecking ball" (Karma 2002, 326) of perestroika, suspecting the end of socialism, and fell into lethargy.

Yet the growing dissonance also had artistic origins. Tamara Danz dismissed most of the lyrics Karma wrote for *Februar* as too unwieldy and roundabout, considering some barely singable. Karma ended up taking back every song but two. His sudden departure left the band faced with a logistical conundrum: With recording already underway, they were missing the words to eight songs. Silly asked a couple of Westerners they respected, among them Rio Reiser, the anarchist singer from Ton Steine Scherben; Nena's Carlo Karges; and singer-songwriter Wolfgang Michels, but couldn't find a common tongue. Tamara Danz harbored literary ambitions of her own and had years' worth of ideas and fragments spread across dozens of notebooks, but didn't see her hour arriving yet as an author skilled enough to match a legacy as powerful as Karma's; she needed an alter ego capable of finding the right metaphors for her feelings. She finally landed on an ideal partner in Gerhard Gundermann, a rock 'n' roll songwriter from Saxony. Gundermann was a forceful, colorful personality, a vociferous and eloquent intellectual who abided by his proletarian roots while keeping up a love-hate relationship with the state as a collaborator and dissident. The authorities refused to issue Gundermann a passport, so while the band recorded their parts in Kreuzberg, he and Tamara Danz raced to finish the rest of the lyrics from East Berlin, less than three miles' distance from the studio as the crow flies, separated by the Wall.

5 The Album

The Visual Concept

Februar came out in West Germany on February 8, 1989, followed two weeks later in the East. While the overall track listing was identical, presentation and marketing varied by country. The difference in approach was most apparent from the cover. The Western version glows cool blue as day breaks in late winter. A grainy image of the band that blurs at the top shows the musicians smiling, already dressed in lighter clothing and looking as though they were on the move. Their candid, relaxed expressions and loose body language convey a feeling of energy and optimism: Let's do this! The center of the image is slightly overexposed, as though the first rays of sun were breaking through. The classic "Silly" signature, a band trademark, has been altered and now beckons with a seductive gold.

The GDR cover registers a completely different mood. It was designed by Jürgen Schmidt-André, a young graphic artist from East Berlin who grew up with the band's music. Schmidt-André opted for a hybrid of painting and drawing, with a stripped-down quality that strikes a contrast to the rich sonic landscape of the album while giving equal weight to its political message. Schmidt-André found initial inspiration in a cassette of rough tracks the band had given him, especially the surreal atmosphere on "Ein Gespenst geht um" [A Specter

Haunts]. He also drew partial aesthetic inspiration from the music video for "Take on Me" by Norwegian pop group a-ha, which captured the musicians' expressions and personality through rough animated illustrations. In searching for a visual language that would set a new accent in Amiga's catalog, it had been important to Schmidt-André to preserve the band's corporate identity. It "had suited [him] just fine that Silly's logo was designed as lettering [of the band name]. It meant that there was something pre-determined to a certain extent, the sense of lightness, haptics, the hand-made. I could work with that. I deliberately ruled out a photographic solution as the most obvious course of action. I wanted to create something special, to allow room for fantasy" (Schmidt-André 2023, interview).

In contrast to the Ariola release, the Amiga cover strikes a decidedly gloomy tone. The stark aesthetic could only be seen as a response to the political writing on the wall, so to speak, and a snub against the perpetual stream of triumphs announced in state propaganda. The band seems to stand in a waiting room, their expressions grave, maybe even resigned. A feeling of farewell lies in the air. A solo acoustic guitar is strummed as though it were the final song; the others have already laid down their instruments. Yet the impression shifts when one puts on the record—now it is resolve that one detects in the image, intransigence. It wasn't the last song the guitarist was strumming; it was the prelude to a deafening scream.

The viewer's gaze is drawn inevitably to Tamara Danz, who is positioned squarely in front at right, though she doesn't dominate the scene. Instead, we get an impression of the band as a single unit bound by oath. At the upper left of the bare room, a pale light falls through an opening, a door or a window, casting fateful reflections across the black-and-white image. A smoldering red spreads across the top and bottom edges of the cover that could be either—a multi-alarm fire threatening disaster, or the reflected light of the sun just breaking out over the horizon. Silly appears again on the back cover of the record in a matchbook-size sketch, smiling. The miniature image provides some comfort, showing the band as they would have been known through countless photos.

In the GDR, *Februar* arrived with an advertising campaign run by Marcus-Macchio-Produktion, a young, independent design agency. The effort focused on printed ephemera like posters or wall calendars based on Jürgen Schmidt-André's graphic work. Three videos were produced in the West for promotion's sake; the first single, "Verlorene Kinder" [Lost Children], clearly had to make do on a tight budget and fell back on all manner of cliché. Cut in between shots of the band sitting idly by in a room are sees images of the big city, the sad high-rise housing projects of Berlin, stands bearing fruit from southern climes, the Wall, streets wet with rain, barren trees, a rat. The video for the second single, "Paradiesvögel" [Birds of Paradise] pursues a more cogent artistic concept; in an otherwise empty circus tent, Silly performs accompanied by trapeze artists, jugglers, and balancing acts. It is the universal dream of freedom, immersed here in intimate semi-darkness, a world of effortlessness and illusion that seems just within reach.

The filmed version of "SOS," meanwhile, narrates an actual moment of contemporary history—the collapse of the GDR. The video moves between Silly playing the song at a rock festival in

Skanderborg in Denmark and aboard a boat on the river Spree in Berlin. The same old militarized border points are there as before, the GDR flag still flies as the shadowy image of head of state Erich Honecker peers out from the gray canyons between apartment buildings. Sequences from the war film *Das Boot* heighten the drama as waves ascend, the roaring sea lashes, and a ship goes down in flames. Revolt crests on the horizon like a force of nature.

Words and Music

Even if the West paid for the production and the album came out in both Germanies, *Februar* primarily drew its following from fans in the GDR. Theirs was the language spoken on the record, and it dealt with subjects that moved them. Many still listen to *Februar* today as a concept album, the "soundtrack to the fall of the GDR" (Könau 2024, 1). In doing so, they point to songs that can be construed as describing the death throes of East Germany—they make up nearly half the record, overshadowing the rest with their strident tone. Yet the album's true subject is far more subtle, existing on a more abstract plane. *Februar* speaks to the *conditio humana* in the modern world, asking about the price of progress. The lyrics pulled from life experiences specific to the GDR only appear as the baneful fruits of "dictatorship" in subsequent distortions; in reality, they comprised a series of insights into human behavior that were unheard of in the West in their urgency and breadth. The universality of the words makes their messages timeless; it is just as easy to read commentaries about the here and now into them as it is to discover thoughts of what is yet to come.

The rich imagery, delivered in a pop format but with dead-on accuracy, gives them tremendous force.

Unlike the lyrics of most rock bands in Western Germany, Silly's were full of allusions, plays on words, and metaphors, serving simultaneously as communication that had to disguise itself from the censors and a conscious means of style. The moment of "incommensurability," in Goethe's words (Eckermann 1916, 100), created space for free association and varying interpretations, allowing listeners to find their own lives reflected in the music and elevating language itself to an artistic medium, ensuring a long shelf life. It was a form of artistry that had been part of the band's DNA since Werner Karma, and made them so beloved in the GDR.

As a team, Tamara Danz and Gerhard Gundermann picked up seamlessly on Karma's poetic instincts—the change is scarcely noticeable, even if there is a shift in accent. It does strike one that Danz sings less from the first person, taking an external view instead. Even so, she never comes across as distanced, more like an observer describing her world. Overall, the intellectual approach comes across as more intelligible than Karma's increasingly metaphysical musings. In Gerhard Gundermann, Danz found someone who supported her own poetic ambitions and linguistic talent, a partner who gave final form to all the fragments and sketches. Mocked in the press as an "eco-fascist" (Osang 1995, 3) for advocating sustainability and humility in life as in art, Gundermann also introduced an environmentalist perspective that resurfaces as an identifiable element throughout the album. The essential role of the lyrics in the band's artistry meant they were printed on the inner sleeve of the record in East and West alike.

Danz's growing creative role came through in the music as well. She is listed as a co-writer on all ten tracks next to keyboardist Ritchie Barton and guitarist Uwe Hassbecker and credited further with the choral arrangements. The singing on *Februar* bears witness to her continued maturation as an interpreter, showcasing tremendous creative will and arresting vocal control. She alternatively shrieks, jeers, begs, and slurs her syllables, building suspense into her phrasing and exploring the full breadth of her range. She personifies a host of disparate characters, going from rebellious, diabolic, or ironic at times to introverted, vulnerable, and despondent at others. The only figure you won't find on the record is the vamp of earlier albums, a figure we would seem better off keeping a safe distance from.

Danz's exceptional singing was flanked by musicianship of equal genius. Silly's musicians were among the best in their line of work, skilled tradesmen of the craft gifted with broad artistic horizons. Ritchie Barton, an essential part of the band's sound since 1982, had played progressive rock, hard rock, and jazz rock in the 1970s. Uwe Hassbecker and bassist Jäcki Reznicek both had previous experience in jazz, soul, and pop, while drummer Herbert Junck had played for years in an acclaimed blues band. Every member of Silly had completed a solid state education in music; Barton, Reznicek, and Junck all studied at conservatory. Like every other GDR band, Silly lived from their live performances, often playing over one hundred gigs a year. This gave the band a great deal of experience on stage, and they easily overshadowed most of their counterparts in the West.

Februar broke new artistic ground but kept the foundation intact, a dialectic of innovation and preservation that had been a hallmark of the band's creative philosophy since the days of *Mont Klamott*. Even as it begged to be danced to, the music had always set a high artistic standard, rich with detail, intricate, full of surprises. The lyrics were conceived in a literary vein; one could get lost just as easily reading them. They may have been intellectual and visionary, but they were never aloof. While the same telltale marks of quality were recognizable on *Februar*, the record represented a new chapter for the group. Silly had never sounded more complex, yet crystal-clear at the same time. Listening on headphones and with the volume turned up loud enough, one is simply overcome by the layers of sound, technical effects, and musical nuances, mesmerized by the pitch-perfect surround sound and dynamic stereo image. Producer Uwe Hoffmann recalled one important source of inspiration:

> We were excited about *Big Generator*, the latest release from the British prog-rock band Yes. It served as a sort of sonic guide, becoming the model for *Februar*. Silly gave me the chance to try something out myself in that direction. That wouldn't have been possible with my other clients. (Hoffmann 2024, interview)

Aside from classics like Steely Dan, Santana, Queen, Frank Zappa, and The Beatles, the musicians in Silly listed Canadian singer Lisa Dalbello, Peter Gabriel, The Tubes, The Fixx, and Pete Townshend's record *White City* as other important points of reference. The fretless bass, a memorable and ubiquitous voice on the album and one of its signature sounds, paid homage to the epochal influence of Jaco Pastorius, Pino Palladino, and Mick Karn. One conspicuous novelty was the massive vocal choruses, which in some cases took up forty-four recording tracks and gave the album its incantatory effect and exceptional drive.

The songs on the record came about in different ways, with a single guitar riff serving as the basis for some tunes and others composed on piano. The rest was teamwork. The band hammered out finer structural points and moments of finesse in extended jam sessions at its practice space, trying out different possibilities, considering the results, then continuing to search for the best solution. In another break with tradition, nearly all the lyrics were written to fit music that was already finished—in Karma's time, the process ran in the reverse order. A few of the songs and arrangements were developed during preproduction at Amiga, before taking final form at Preußen Tonstudio in West Berlin.

At Work in the Studio

Februar is both—a musical and lyrical milestone, and a masterpiece of production and engineering. The album operated at a level unattainable in the GDR. Amiga had expertly trained staff, but it lacked modern, digital equipment, nor did it have enough hard currency to buy it from the West. Preußen Tonstudio, on the other hand, operated by international standards. The studio was founded in 1981 by Uwe Hoffmann and David Heilmann, two music enthusiasts just turned twenty who played drums and guitar in the West Berlin punk scene. Hoffmann later joined The Other Ones, a pop group that drew international attention for a short stint. As a producer Hoffmann had his breakthrough collaborating with immensely popular punk trio Die Ärzte. Of his time with Silly, he recalled

> taking it as an honor that they asked me. They're fantastic musicians, and quickly became good friends as well. There was a clear division of labor though. As a producer, I always pursue my own taste, my ideas and visions, and that was no different with Silly. Then there was the responsibility I had toward the customer, the record label. Small things that seemed out of place to me were corrected, individual arrangements, harmonies, or the beat. I straightened and pruned, trying to find the right form. (ibid.)

Uwe Hoffmann's creative touch went beyond recording the music on *Februar*, extending to the computer programming, help with arrangements, and handling postproduction. David Heilmann served as the sound engineer. In Silly, they found comrades-in-arms who were not only virtuosos on their instruments but shared a penchant for technology. For nights on end, Ritchie Barton fiddled alongside Hoffmann on the sound and programming. Barton brought high-quality equipment of his own into the studio, including a Teisco SX-400 synthesizer, a Roland D-50, Roland JX-10, and a Roland S-50 mono sampler complete with a sound library. Uwe Hassbecker brought in his collection of guitars and pedalboards with a profusion of effects.

The fretless bass that appears on most tracks has a special story behind it. As Jäcki Reznicek recalled, "in the 1980s I doctored a cheap Fender Jazz Bass copy, it was a Luxor from West Germany. I removed the frets and filled in the grooves, and put on a different pickup. The instrument looked almost like a Jaco Pastorius bass. It had practically no sustain, but a totally unique sound" (Reznicek 2023, interview). Both the GDR musicians' technical ability and their equipment were compatible with the West; the former went by international standards, while the latter had been procured on the black market. Where communication was concerned, though, hurdles arose. David Heilmann recalled that the "musical terminology and jargon were completely different in the East. Silly used terms like 'concert bass drum' for the kick or 'Charleston Machine' for the hi-hat; they spoke in terms of *crescendo* and *ritardando*. I didn't understand a single word the first three days. Zero. We didn't speak the same language. To say nothing of the song lyrics" (Heilmann 2024, interview).

Recording at Preußen Tonstudio was analog, assisted by digital technology. The studio relied on high-quality microphones like Neumann and Shure, two 24-track tape machines in the Otari MTR-90 and MTR-100, and a DDA AMR 24 for a mixing desk. Other core equipment included an Atari computer with the Notator sequencing program; various samplers, among them the Emulator III, Emax, and Akai S1000; a Roland TR-808 "Rhythm Composer" drum machine; the Lexicon 480L reverb unit; and a plethora of effects devices, equalizers, and compressors. The studio was just under 3,000 square feet, housed in a former factory floor with solid room acoustics. One floor below, musician and producer Thommy

Hein ran a smaller studio that was also enlisted in recording. Dieter Ortlepp, who had done the sound engineering for Silly's earlier Amiga records and was allowed to travel to Kreuzberg to observe, described the setup: "Tamara fine-tuned her vocals there while the band was working. She had a sixteen-track tape machine with an info-mix and would try out different options, working out a strategy for herself. When she went back up to the main studio, it was pretty clear how she was going to sing her parts" (Ortlepp 2024, interview).

Producing *Februar* was a time-consuming, complicated process. It pushed the envelope of technical possibilities, which were much more limited than today. The computers and samplers had a minuscule memory, for example, while the lack of a total-recall function meant that settings had to be photographed with a Polaroid camera for the following day. Even today, the band's excitement over the new digital technologies and the potential of a modern studio reverberates when listening to the record. Uwe Hassbecker concurred: "A lot of stuff came out in the production, because we were constantly experimenting. Uwe Hoffmann had to hit the brakes for us some times, saying 'Why don't you do less for a change!' Critics today might find the record overly fussy, too bombastic or cold. But that's how it was back then" (Hassbecker 2023, interview). If one looks for it, it's also possible to detect a continuation in the notion of "progressive" in the production, which had entered rock discourse two decades before and undergone a renaissance and reevaluation since the early 1980s with the MIDI revolution, through a younger generation of musicians and albums like Yes's *90125*. Now, alongside the elaborate, baroque architecture of the compositions, eclectic playing styles, and virtuosic musicianship, digital progress had joined in disclosing previously unknown realms of experience.

Typical of *Februar* is a nuanced sound comprising many layers. There are virtually no blank spaces; everything has been filled in. To achieve this effect, Silly made temporary mixes throughout production; finished analog tracks and keyboard MIDI parts were grouped, then bounced onto a temporary stereo mix, freeing up tape tracks for further recording. The massive choral parts, sung almost entirely by Tamara Danz and Ritchie Barton, wouldn't have been possible without the trick. Once finished, they were imported into the Akai S1000 as a cappella stereo mixes, then added to the analog tracks by MIDI trigger.

The rhythmic elements of the record similarly came together piece by piece. Herbert Junck's drumming appears on half of the songs, with some sampled and edited on the computer by Uwe Hoffmann. The rest Hoffmann programmed after the fact, using Junck's sounds as a basis then playing it himself on an Octapad. Percussion effects from the Roland TR-808 and the sampler's sound library further elevated rhythmic tension throughout the record. All keyboards, acoustic piano included, were recorded as MIDI data into the sequencer, which worked in sync mode as a slave. Only the Hammond B3 with its Leslie speaker, as appears on "SOS" and "Traumteufel," and the analog synthesizer Teisco SX-400, were miked in standard fashion and recorded to tape. Devices used in production were synchronized by SMPTE timecode; a click track was used to set the tempo of the songs.

Song by Song

Februar hails from an era in pop music history when albums were still listened to from A to Z, as complete works unto themselves. The dramaturgy of the album—released on vinyl and cassette in the GDR, and in the West on CD as well—took account of that fact, setting the harder material on the album next to quieter, more introverted numbers or poppier sounds to cushion the blow, and keeping the subjects in flux. The record's complex melodic gestures and aesthetic consistency hold the listener spellbound from beginning to end, maintaining an overall impression of unity even with its more experimental elements, and continuing to project energy, drive, and restlessness in more collected moments. *Februar* can be listened to any number of ways—as intellectual edification or an invitation to dance.

Ein Gespenst geht um—A Specter Haunts

The Western and Eastern versions of *Februar* had different openings. In the West, Ariola decided against "Ein Gespenst geht um," feeling its vocabulary to be overly specific to the GDR, and went instead with the catchier "Verlorene Kinder," which also came out as a single. The marketing decision interfered with the album's carefully conceived narrative, rattling the foundation to a certain extent. In the chorus of the Amiga opener, Tamara Danz scornfully sings "A specter's haunting Mitropa / it moves about the graveyard of dreams." The words carried tremendous associative power in the GDR, referencing the famous opening lines from Karl Marx and Friedrich Engels' *Communist Manifesto*, which every GDR student had to read in school: "A specter is haunting Europe—the specter of Communism" (Marx and Engels 1974, 78). Now, however, the revolutionary spirit had descended into the station pubs run by Mitropa, East Germany's rail system, the epitome of dreck and despair, a parallel world of the stranded.

The song is fit to bursting with metaphor, plays on words, turns of phrase. The very first line, "The dimwit clown reads out the paper," held powerful enough resonance for GDR fans, recalling the empty phrases of politicians, the opportunists and closed minds, and referencing in "the paper" a medium of lies that was forever being satirized in the visual arts, film, and cabaret of the GDR. Symbols of collapse and the end thread through the song, a "tiger with dentures," "the ballerina with a bald patch," "the laid-off circus clown." Only the "tired flower-power hippie" playing the Russian "balalaika" to the tune of Glasnost is offered as a respite before the final catastrophe. "The dimwit clown" who nobody listens to anymore finally folds his newspaper into an airplane; he remains cut off from reality. Fresh disaster looms on the horizon, an ecological apocalypse that will swallow everything: "The good lord beat it long ago / since he had nothing left to do."

The wealth of lyrical imagery is matched by a compelling, layered sound that on headphones is nearly claustrophobic in effect. The vocal choruses especially make their presence felt. Used throughout the track to the point of excess and assigned a prominent place in the mix, they pile up over dozens of recording tracks, filling every last corner of the sonic space. The choruses are much more than simply acoustic finesse; they comment on and parody the lyrics, sinking sarcastic barbs into the flesh. Onomatopoeic syllables are repeated with a sort of gallows humor that more properly belongs in the realm of the ridiculous or infantile. Tamara Danz similarly tends to undercut the lyrics with her singing, declaiming at times like a children's storyteller before twisting her voice and doubling it an octave up, or raising it into a vulgar shout. A guitar lurches along sounding out a tritone, the "Devil's interval" condemned by the medieval church as demonic and blasphemous. The bass prances about from one foot to the other like a court jester, a trumpet sample ruffles its feathers, while the drums whip the entire miserable troop along ahead of it. This is a specter that no longer needs to be feared. It is only a shadow of itself, and will crumble to dust with the first light of the approaching spring.

"Ein Gespenst geht um" gives us a fitting introduction to the world of *Februar*, setting the lyrical and musical frame for the entire record and pulling out all the production stops. The band also manages artistic tribute by incorporating a brief sample from Yes's hit "Owner of a Lonely Heart."

Verlorene Kinder—Lost Children

The second song stands in marked contrast to the opener. The structure is clearer and it dispenses with the dissonant tension; a catchy refrain with sweeping melodic arcs and an elegant appeal suggests itself for pop radio. Warm, natural sounds whisk us away into a world of longing, a sitar drawing us eastward among tablas, exotic glissando effects, and syncopated percussion. Another Indian instrument, the bowed sarangi, appears later in the song. The instruments sound deceptively real, though they all come from the sound library. They are joined by a sonorous fretless bass and guitars recorded to tape, adding a southern flair and sense of wanderlust to the track. The bass is recorded onto multiple tracks and plays the third and fifth of the chord instead of the root, elevating harmonic tension. "Small, rhythmic Jaco Pastorius elements" (Reznicek 2023, interview) placed out in front in the mix evoke the longings of the heart. Subdued synthesized strings convey a feeling of floating while a piano twirls about Tamara Danz's voice, which is unaffected and penetrating. Nothing here is relativized or undercut ironically; the song tells a straightforward story.

It sings of "the lost children / on the streets of Berlin," whether East or West is left for the listener to decide. Both sides of the city knew the hopelessness of cold, concrete silos crouched in the twilight "like an evil beast." The children freeze, dreaming of "warm lands" where they would "like to flee." The lines were especially incendiary in the GDR, since they brushed up against the sacrilege of *Republikflucht*, desertion of the republic, a crime punishable by law. In an East German studio, the verb "flee" itself wouldn't have gotten past the censors. The idea of breaking away finds its acoustic counterpart in the bridge, where the instruments almost seem to flood the stereo channels. Overall, the deliberate, subtle panning gives the song a riveting panoramic sound, reminding us of how wide the world really is.

Alle gegen einen—All Against One

In a second deviation from the original track order, the third song on the Western version is "Landekreuz auf meiner Seele," another pop song that tells an individual love story. The third track on the Amiga release, "Alle gegen einen," picks up on a universal theme—the ancient lust for bread and circuses—flipping the motto "one for all and all for one" from Alexandre Dumas's *The Three Musketeers* on its head in the process. In the chorus, we hear: "Always everybody against the one / and one against it all / always everybody on their feet / and one that takes the fall." We sit in a Spanish arena and listen to the thoughts of the bull addressing the torero, a victim just like the bull, though he doesn't seem to realize. He aims his sword for the animal's heart as the "mob" thunders, "they clap till they've got nothing left / and I'm supposed to dance." It is the perfidious game that power plays, dazzling the masses and plying them with cheap thrills so it can rule according to its wishes. In the end, the bull asks from beyond the grave, "How badly off do they have to be / in this very moment / to want to see somebody die / just to survive."

The song opens with a sinewy funk riff on guitar played to a drum track with short reverb. After a single castanet hit, a keyboard fanfare that will serve as a leitmotif and a syncopated, driving fretless bass line enter. A Flamenco guitar dispels all doubt as to our location. Tamara Danz's voice reflects the gravity of the situation, now sounding melancholy and withdrawn in the mix, now aggressive and dramatic, though maintaining a sense of dignity throughout. It is especially affecting that a woman has taken on the role of the sacrificial animal, and gives the song yet another layer of meaning as an implied battle of the sexes. The soundscape and spectrum of styles grows in complexity in the instrumental bridge as the doomed bull rears once more. We hear Gospel piano, distorted space guitars, and "progressive" rock. The intended audience really is universal.

SOS

A furious guitar riff kicks off the next track, and one senses immediately that everything is on the line. The band isn't playing for kicks; it's playing as a means of revolt. "SOS" is the only straightforward rock song on *Februar*, guitar-driven, fast, unswerving, and dynamic, and pulling the listener helplessly along. The same emphasis permeates the lyrics, whose political bent is clearer here than anywhere else on the record. For an East German listener, it is obvious that hers is the country being described as headed for catastrophe. The GDR is a battered ship bound for a watery grave, a leaky Titanic with mutiny afoot. Metaphors of decline and ruin surface throughout: a "black reef," an "iceberg," and a "second-hand ship of fools" with a "ship orchestra" to keep spirits afloat. Even so, the image remains ambivalent, offering glimpses of hope: "Still the engine powers forward / plows full steam ahead / still the cafeteria hands out / free daily bread." The crew clings to what they were promised when they signed on: "still we dream of coming home / and believe the captain."

A singular tension runs through the song lyrics, the rumble of protest. The infernal group chant of "SOS" in the choruses contains a gloomy sense of foreboding, just like the steady repetition of the phrase "immer noch," which translates as "still" but with greater emphasis, as if to ask "how much longer until?" Danz skewers passengers who choose to overlook the impending shipwreck as they "graze and gulp and gulp and graze," abandoning themselves to fatalistic decadence. The piano hammers while the bassist plucks at the strings with a vengeance, delivering a funky line with commanding punch. Before the final verse the guitar lifts off for a spectacular solo that spirals upward in perfect time, firing off feverish sixteenth notes like a machine gun salvo. Then the band sets the fuse to the powder keg: "Still the light burns till four in the morning / down inside the boiler room / Still we haven't got the key / to the ammunition room." Tamara Danz shouts the final line of the song with genuine rage and ardor before the SOS call rings out once more. This is rebellion plain and simple, distilled into word and sound.

Über ihr taute das Eis—Above Her the Ice Set to Thaw

Many fans join the band in considering the last song on the A-side to be the album's centerpiece, its most emotional and stirring number. Classification zealots would likely file the song away under "power ballad," since it lacks any trace of sentimentality. A woman, still young we assume, stands along the shores of a frozen lake. The ice has already begun to melt; warmer weather beckons. Yet her mind is made up; she doesn't want to live anymore. The listener's heart clenches; the suicide seems completely unnecessary. What happened?

At surface level, the lyrics follow a girl who "froze among people." Even after her death the others remain cold. When the body is pulled from the lake, people "marvel" at her "smiling lips." Is it an expression of triumph, or final release? The rescue team is scandalized: "Where will we end up / if there are people smiling / beyond the borders of our world." The girl is given a quick burial, and "order was restored." In the final verse, the next victim stands on the shore. It is the singer herself, who repeats the start of the song in the first person.

Werner Karma, who wrote the lyrics, denies standard interpretations of the song: "I'm not writing about a person who goes to ruin because of the GDR. My intention was different" (Karma 2023, interview). Rather, it is his commentary on the policies of Mikhail Gorbachev, who Karma didn't take to be a "new God and redeemer" but a "skinner" (Karma 2002, 326). "The girl symbolizes socialism saying goodbye before the spring arrives. Nobody got that" (Karma 2023, interview).

The song opens dramatically, with swelling cymbals and a glassy guitar that appears throughout the record, though here it comes to the fore. The guitar was partially run straight into the mixing console through special compressors and effects and then given rhythmic delay, resulting in a sound with a carrying density that was still uncommon at the time. It is played with a hard attack and picked cleanly, the delay and stereo effects bringing to mind waves rippling out in concentric circles. We are gazing down into icy, clear water, a bottomless grave. Tamara Danz strikes up a dirge that carries a pitch of intensity unique to the album. Producer Uwe Hoffmann explains:

> After a hard day's work in West Berlin we hit the bars and partied for a bit. It must have been around four in the morning or so, when all of a sudden Tamara said "I want to sing now." So we drove back to the studio. Tamara got up on the mic and sang "Über ihr taute das Eis." I will never forget that moment, it still touches me today. I believe the song reflects the intimate

> atmosphere, the city asleep, studio empty, Tamara diving into another world with her eyes closed. (Hoffmann 2024, interview)

The kaleidoscopic moods of the track, which fluctuate between despair, resolve, and the assuredness of eternal rest, are underscored by harmonic shifts that far exceed pop music standards. The second verse opens with a drastic chord change as the woman breaks off from the shoreline, moving from $F^{\#5}$ and $C^{\#m7}/E$ to F^{6}/A and G^{sus4}/A. We know there's no holding her back anymore, feel the ice breaking up. Danz's voice rises in pain as the lifeless body is recovered, the fretless bass weeping along. Voice sounds played on the keyboard and a floating guitar give the chorus a lustrous quality, as Danz sings "frozen among people / she grew warm again / as she dropped between the fish / and above her the ice set to thaw." Drum breaks echo the emotional turmoil, vocal slides the worry. If one removes the acoustic patina from the chorus and reduces it to its harmonic structure, one would be left with the choral parts of a requiem. The song returns to its central message as it fades out, insistently repeating "above her the ice set to thaw"—whether due to the human warmth of the girl, or the sun as it returns, is left to the listener's imagination.

Traumteufel—Dream Devil

The B-side of *Februar* opens with "Traumteufel," a song that rivals the A-side opener "Ein Gespenst geht um" in its breadth of sound and wealth of metaphors. We awaken gradually with a fade-in, the notes of the bass recalling the breath of a sleeper as a guitar pattern spirals out of the depths of the subconscious. Rhythmic shifts imitate an irregular heartbeat trying to steady itself from a nightmare; the snare drum is syncopated ahead of the beat, making the meter hard to find. A wall of guitars rises up to meet the listener, a Hammond organ snarls; a sense of nervousness hovers in the air. As if in a trance, Tamara Danz delivers her vision: "I had a dream / the Kaiser was long dead / now it's just his double on the throne / he looks good / though he's a bonehead / and loves to fiddle with the red telephone." The lyrics inevitably lead to thoughts of the geriatrics in GDR leadership, and the next generation of upstarts already waiting in the wings, likely to do more harm than good.

The next verse goes a step further, seemingly anticipating the fall of the Wall. We're confronted with an image of collapse and capitulation: "I had a dream / the iron hand / that keeps on grubbing up the ground / is now out of work / 'cause everything has been burned / to light the neon signs in the golden town." Fears of ecological armageddon flare again; the "minister" finds himself unable to laugh "since the woods no longer knew / how to grow leaves." He abandons hope and hangs himself "by the desk."

An oppressive sense of foreboding takes hold in the dark hours of the night. Yet then, dawn breaks: "The radio man wakes me up / he kisses me and boils me an egg." We are reminded of some sunny advertising jingle that would like us to believe "Folgers is the best part of waking up." The "dream devil" slinks off with an impish *addio mon amour*, neither a demon nor an enemy as it turns out, but a guard at the gates of truth. The bright new reality that the happy-go-lucky radio dangles before us, meanwhile, has been polished to shine and trimmed to fit; it leads us around like we were marionettes. The deceptive shine of the chorus is supported by an exultant guitar that repeats the song's opening riff on loop, leaping octaves to burn out in distorted harmonics. Layer by layer, the sound forms an impenetrable thickness; we find other guitar tracks and styles nested inside each other, keyboards, a percussive jingle, vocal choruses, and a conventional e-bass rounded off with punchy fretless fill-ins. They storm their way forward impetuously, overpowering even the singer. The sonic orgy finally dissipates in a fade-out as we sink back into sleep. Yet the nightmare is far from over.

Landekreuz auf meiner Seele—Touchdown on my Soul

The time has come for the album's first love song. A mysterious rustle of chimes and atonal piano improvisation usher us into a narrow, winding space. Hesitantly feeling our way through, we wonder what lies around the bend. A computerized drum pulses. The smoke and mirrors dissipate with the third hand clap and a beguiling pop song takes us under its spell. The sound of a marimba emanates tropical warmth while the guitar, clearer and more concise than usual, develops an ostinato figure, yearning, pleading.

Tamara Danz narrates the end of a love affair from a strong female perspective. Her partner has emptied his dresser and scribbled a final message "on the stained mirror," yet she won't give up on him; she "sets the dammed house on fire" and follows his "tracks." Her love is selfless, stronger than any indignities suffered. In the chorus, Danz sings "The touchdown on my soul / still lies open for you / and if your tank empties / on the way to your star / turn 'round and call out for me." Danz's voice is doubled several times over and shines forth over broad melodic arcs, communicating an irrepressible force and resolve. The song is articulating an elemental connection between two kindred spirits, not some passing fancy.

An instrumental interlude betrays the stormy emotions at play; the slap bass and funk guitar compete with one another, kindling a hopeful passion. The next and final verse stands open to interpretation: "I stand in the last house on earth / my dead-tired heart, flickers in hand." Spontaneously, we might think of giving up in discouragement if it weren't for the sinewy rhythm of the drums and heated guitar arpeggios. They transform the lines into their opposite, signaling an unbroken will. A second bridge led by cool jazz piano gives us a moment's pause before the touchdown lights up again. We end on "soul," the key to the song. Tamara Danz sings it on the subdominant, drifting off into eternity. We know now how to read the searching introduction. While the basic questions of human relationships may sound straightforward, they are anything but.

Alles wird besser—It's All Getting Better

A furious hit on the drums yanks us out of our brooding and back into reality; synthetic horns and unnerving guitars grab us by the scruff and race ahead without loosening their grip. The reckoning draws nigh. Tamara Danz flips open the register of sins, we can sense her piercing gaze. She is cool and provocative, singing in the plural. We all stand without exception on the list of the accused, faced with facts we would much rather repress. The lyrics attest to our boundless greed and egotism, which we keep concealed behind rank hypocrisy. We couldn't care less about tomorrow, "after us, the flood!" We worship the delusion of growth like an idol, the insane logic of better-faster-stronger that is driving our planet to ruin. "We want Mother Nature / we want gasoline / and paranormal / energy / we want to be pretty / and smart as well / but no matter what / we want to be rich enough." The chorus tosses the price scornfully in our faces: "It's all getting better / but it won't turn out well."

Then as now, the song comes as a reckoning with the ruthlessness and arrogance of the Western world. Werner Karma, who wrote the lyrics, nevertheless maintains its East German perspective: "That was a GDR song. The state tried more and more to buy people, to bind them through consumption. With imported cars, boutique food shops, or pop music. But it was a hopeless race" (Karma 2023, interview). From this vantage point, the "soft cuddly charms" everyone wants, the "aerosol can" and "underground overseas pornos," take on a different connotation. They are the purported blessings of Western freedom that likewise served as the measure of all things in the GDR, and which over the long term eroded the vision of socialism in East Germany.

The music lays out our false beliefs and corruptible natures by ironic means. It is both—irresistible and distressing. The horns sound artificial, snorting and spluttering as though scarcely able to contain their laughter. Staccato marimba samples race out from beneath our wrathful grasping, chuckling like goblins, while the keyboard performs atonal pirouettes. The guitars stagger ahead, hoaxing us with the endlessly repeating intro riff. Tamara Danz wrenches her voice, shouting spitefully and rolling her Rs in a highly affected delivery. As if that weren't enough she asks us to sing along, her voice panning to the back of the right channel to allow space. The drums egg us on with an animating rhythm, inviting listeners to clap along. After four minutes class is dismissed, fizzling out with a subsiding trumpet sound, like a balloon deflating. We've gotten away once more.

Männer wollen Frauen—Men Want Women

The opening of the next song misleads us. A vaguely Latin rhythm invites a sense of ease and a conga drum calls us to dance, yet tragedy lies in store. We're introduced to a female character we've met once before in "So 'ne kleine Frau" [Such a Little Lady], an earlier hit from 1985's *Liebeswalzer*. Her luck with men wasn't any better back then either, life a sad succession of one-night stands. As we meet again, the years of searching and disappointment have left their mark. She's grown quieter, more reticent. Earlier the spark of desire was quick to catch; these days her body stays cold. She doesn't feel anything when she is pushed "through the cool cushions"; nobody can find her "start switch." And still she tries. We hear the chorus and sense the pointlessness: "And you paint yourself up like a clown / but it's for an empty tent / every man wants a woman / does anybody want you anymore?" The rhetorical question lingers in the air.

Tamara Danz sings in the second person, maintaining distance as an observer yet staying wholly empathetic. As the full scope of the tragedy unfurls, the song switches from B^5 in the third verse to Em^6/G and $Fis^{7/sus4}$ in the fourth. "Hammered" now, the protagonist hooks up with a young, inexperienced man. Finally she's able to let herself go, carried off on the wings of desire: "You led his hand around / that made you hot / he didn't do it with you / so you did it with him." As she repeats the line Danz's voice falters, leaving out the second phrase. The "heat" is gone and disillusionment sets back in; even a scene that seems so close to satisfaction ends in resignation. A guitar soars into a high, distorted register, unleashing its despair. The fretless bass sighs. Tamara Danz sings a duet with herself, tossed to and fro in the swirl of emotions. The song closes with a second guitar solo, more elegiac than the first, before finally falling immobile in a long sustain. Who knows whether we'll find the same woman back in the spotlight again.

Paradiesvögel—Birds of Paradise

The feathery rhythm of drum brushes against a snare triggers a search reflex—what's the source of the fluttering? Our gaze wanders about the room until we catch sight of him—a splendid, iridescent bird flying in circles. A counter rhythm arrives played on the claves, and with a single triangle hit the singer enters. A lively 6/8 waltz sweeps us along as we begin to twirl about in our mind's eye. Tamara Danz holds a dialogue with her alter ego, a bird of paradise who opens her eyes before disappearing through the window. His weightless circling inspires thoughts of freedom, anarchy, toppling old illusions. The masks fall from friends that only appear as such; the "posters" of fame decorating Tamara Danz's "room" grow "pale," her "dream kingdom" bursts "into shards." While it may sound like a cautionary tale, the chorus is intended as encouragement: "Birds of paradise can't be kept caged / they need all the sky up above, just one part is too small." Shouldn't we give it a try ourselves?

Compared to the other songs on *Februar*, the song stands out for its clear, coherent structure and cathartic harmony. The keyboards sound at times like an entire film orchestra, rolling the silver screen down before us. The reverb on the programmed rhythm tracks evokes a large room, while chorus effects give the fretless bass a weightless warmth. A mellow guitar disguised through a Leslie speaker holds us captive over the bridge, as an elaborate soundscape recalls the bewitching avian world; the whirr of hummingbirds or the majestic gait of the cassowary. The song offers images of redemption and peace triumphing over the trials and tribulations of winter. *Februar* ends with the optimism of a major key. We're ready for spring.

6 Resonance

Pro and Contra in the GDR

Like all Silly albums, *Februar* landed with a splash in East Germany. The record sold 91,000 copies in the first three months alone, many times what other bands were able to report. Mainstream GDR rock had been in existential crisis for years with both its relevance and audience dwindling. A new generation had long since departed for the West psychologically and punished East Germany's rock acts for being state lackeys. Silly, City, and Pankow were the exceptions; their music had a modern sound, and the lyrics contained a certain fire.

Februar would never have appeared in the form it did had the political authorities had their way. The record's message plainly crossed the tolerance threshold. Yet unlike before, this time efforts at censorship ran aground. Keyboardist Ritchie Barton recalled one pivotal scene:

> The head of Amiga René Büttner came to Preußen Tonstudio to approve the record. A long moment of silence followed after we listened to the production, before Büttner said "But you can't do that!" To which Tamara simply replied "Bütti, the record is done." Period! Some of the lyrics Büttner was hearing for the first time, since they had been written while recording. The East had lost control, its grip on things, it was presented

> with a fait accompli. Ariola would have put the record out come what may, and would even have drawn marketing capital from a ban. So the functionaries had to eat humble pie. (Barton 2023, interview)

A second attempt failed just as miserably. The general director of Mitropa filed a complaint about the harmful impact that the song "Ein Gespenst geht um" would have on business, and demanded *Februar* be taken off the market by temporary court injunction. To Tamara Danz, it was

> obvious that it came from above, they were just looking for someone to give the thing a sheen of legality. Shortly before trial, it was brought to their attention that Ariola's seat of jurisdiction was in Munich—in other words, it would cost them a small fortune in Western cash, since it would be hard for them to get away with. So that died too. (Stolle 1993, 12)

A more unequivocal declaration of bankruptcy was hard to imagine; "ideology capitulated before the power of money" (Danz 1997a, 209).

The sounds of the state gnashing and grinding its teeth echoed periodically in the press. Before, Silly records had been considered sacrosanct, eliciting unanimous praise; now, rumbles of dissent mixed in with the applause. A few newspapers ran multiple reviews at the same time, setting the positive alongside the negative to give the impression of a balanced conflict of opinion, though in truth it was merely to coat a bitter pill in sham democratic pretenses. The lyrics were taken to task for their "distance," for lacking a "productive stance" (Heinze 1989, 5), their East-West "vacillations" (Thomas

1989, 10) and "pessimistic worldview" (Jachmann 1989, 3). "Why is it that Silly no longer takes a more active, engaged approach toward life?" (ibid.) Musically speaking as well, *Februar* resembled a "pile of glass shards," leaving one pining for "melodies that fell easy on the ear" (ibid). The response to the hit "Verlorene Kinder" was allergic—did the band mean to suggest that this sort of social deprivation and wanderlust existed in the GDR? To do so wouldn't simply be "unfair," it would completely bypass reality (ibid). Tamara Danz and Gerhard Gundermann ought to have made it unmistakably clear that they could only have West Berlin in mind, where one encountered similar fates at every corner. First among the "lost children" were the daughters and sons of Turkish guest workers, who eked out a meager existence on the streets of Kreuzberg while longing for their home in the south (see Günter 1989, 5).

The highbrow and specialist press, previously given over to fits of enthusiasm every time a Silly record came out, kept a similar distance. Instead, they passed judgment from on high, madly enough accusing songs that had so ingeniously captured the signs of the times of "observations that hadn't been adequately processed and lacked sufficient depth," and "simplified problems" (Lange 1989, 13). Perhaps the authors didn't want to wind up burning their fingers on what had turned out to be a hot potato; all of them certainly took exception to the band parting ways with Werner Karma and the musicians' new self-confidence.

Unreservedly positive opinions were few and far between. Radio host Lutz Bertram, who had blessed the band with regular airplay (all while abusing their trust as a Stasi operative) didn't detect any flaws. He credited Silly with speaking to wakeful minds "from the heart," and finding that "*Februar* didn't come across as opportunistic unease or teary-eyed contrition about the 'circumstances'; I sooner had a feeling that the band was looking forward to a period of change with a sense of ease" (Bertram 1989, 38 and 39). A similar tenor ran through readers' letters to the weekly newspaper *Sonntag*, which put three different reviews of the album up for discussion. Unlike the journalists who played fault-finder only to wind up in a colorless stalemate, the fans took up cudgels for the band. *Februar* was downright "addictive"; the record embodied "something totally new, contentious, and energizing that wasn't available yet in our record shops" (Löhr 1989, 2). The song lyrics "were so explosive, sparking layer after layer of associations, that it is breathtaking in the truest sense of the word" (Bicher 1989, 2).

Reactions in West Germany

The same sort of interpretive struggles formed no part of the West German reaction. Tamara Danz and her band were received with arms wide open, hailed as a new star rising in the East. Once popular imports like the Puhdys "now elicited only a tired yawn," now coming across as "really fully outdated" (Scholz 1989, 10). Silly, on the other hand, stood on the cusp of the era and were anything but provincial—you couldn't tell their actual origins. *Februar* was celebrated as a "passionate rock album with a fiery concoction of funk and hard rock ingredients." At times the lyrics evidenced "truly snotty linguistic wit" (ibid.). After thirteen days of shows in the

GDR in April 1989, the band set out through West Germany and Austria on its "Verlorene Kinder" tour. A reviewer from the opening concert raved about the "absolute strength of the musicians," giving readers his word of honor that "if you don't know Silly by now, you're missing out" (Tiger 1989, 14).

Overall, Western media was less interested in music criticism or exegesis than the political aura surrounding this group from the East, who had made such a racket clambering over the Wall. Silly balked at the skewed focus, as they explained in the press kit assembled by Ariola:

> We would like, just for once, to sit for an interview that's just about the music. It isn't like Bruce Springsteen is constantly being asked why he lives in the U.S. We live here because we grew up here, our friends are here, and because in the end all the crap—political and social—balances out no matter where you live. But here we know precisely what it is we have to fight for or against. That's what we learned through all our travels. (BMG Ariola 1989)

Tamara Danz and Uwe Hassbecker defended this same credo late in March 1989, in conversation with GDR rock expert Olaf Leitner on a show broadcast on West Germany's RIAS station entitled "Traveling Blunts Illusions." In Leitner's opinion, *Februar* "didn't necessarily contain subjects specific to the GDR" but addressed problems that were universal to the modern "industrial state" with its "baseline tendency toward depression," thus aiming at a "transnational market." Leitner was corrected by the musicians—the messages in the songs drew exclusively on the East German experience, and the things that came up in the songs "were playing out in the GDR." Danz also set the record straight regarding readings of "Verlorene Kinder" that mistakenly placed the song in Kreuzberg: "We don't write tunes about the West since we're a GDR band, and we're describing our own circumstances" (Leitner 1989).

The authorities in East Berlin took painstaking note of Silly's appearances in Western media, chafing at any politically inflected utterances. One long article published in March 1989 in *Stern*, a high-circulation West German weekly, verged on catastrophe. At a Silly show in Frankfurt an der Oder in Brandenburg, the Western journalists had been impressed by the large police presence arranged for them. The piece described how the musicians greeted the Stasi directly from the stage, and otherwise didn't mince words in the interview when discussing censorship, East German crimes against the environment, dissidents, the ray of hope Gorbachev brought, and the coldness of the West. Drummer Herbert Junck attacked head of state Erich Honecker, expressing the shame he felt at Honecker's statement that the Wall would still be standing a hundred years from now (Lahann 1989, 138). A large-format band photo crowned the provocation: It showed Silly standing stony-faced in front of the Brandenburg Gate, on the boundary line between East and West. You could almost hear "SOS" playing in the background.

When the heretical piece came out on March 30, 1989, Tamara Danz took the bull by the horns. It was clear enough to her and the other musicians that retribution loomed, with the upcoming tour in the West on the line. On April 2, a Sunday, Danz placed a private call to Hartmut König—a figure she had known from their early days together at the Oktoberklub, since

Figure 6.1 *Silly in 1989 at the Brandenburg Gate in East Berlin, from the photo session for the article in* Stern, *14/1989. From left: Ritchie Barton, Herbert Junck, Jäcki Reznicek, Tamara Danz, Thomas Fritzsching, Uwe Hassbecker © Karin Rocholl.*

risen to deputy cultural minister—and requested to meet in confidence. The appointment took place the very next day, in the office of the department head of Entertainment Arts. Silly protested its innocence, accusing *Stern* of prejudiced, warped reporting. Their statements had been taken out of context, and they had been denied a chance to authorize their quotes. Notes from the meeting further highlighted the fact that "the band were only ever asked about political problems, despite repeatedly insisting—in writing as well—throughout their conversations [with *Stern*] and other press interviews that they wanted to respond to questions about their profession and music, and not political matters" (Zabel 1989a, 149). The functionaries believed the band's account and they emerged unscathed, though just barely. When risky new statements came to light, the culture ministry summoned the artists and their manager back in May 1989, this time threatening "legal consequences" and the cancellation of their travel visas. Ultimately, there were "no allowances for media activities of that sort" (Zabel 1989b).

Noisy headlines notwithstanding, sales of *Februar* in the West lagged behind Ariola's expectations. When compared to Amiga's balance sheets, the West German figures almost looked like a flop. Still, Ariola boss Thomas Stein kept his faith in Silly, predicting a rosy future for the band at the album's unveiling in Munich and declaring "it our intention to build the group systematically from the ground up" (cited in Balitzki 1989, 29). But things took an unexpected turn. When the Wall came down, marketing interests shifted; the goal now was to make Silly presentable as a pop group and water down the content of the songs. The band reached for the escape hatch, ending their contract with Ariola. In 1996 they took off for one last artistic flight, releasing the CD *Paradies [Paradise]* independently.

7 Play It Back

The Final Days of the GDR

Over the summer 1989, the songs on *Februar* start to take on a life of their own. They're no longer listened to as foreboding prophecy, but actual commentary on the spiraling political crisis in the GDR. Popular discontent with a government that remains completely cut off from reality has grown louder; thousands flee West across the by-now porous border between Hungary and Austria, while others force their way out by occupying West German embassies in East Berlin, Budapest, Prague, and Warsaw. SED leadership twists the facts of the matter, sending former GDR citizens on their way with a sneer: "With their behavior every one of them has trampled our moral values and shut themselves out of our society. We needn't shed a tear on their behalf" (ADN 1989, 2).

The insularity of those in power elevated art's power as a communicative means of correction and criticism. Like many others, Silly used the stage to speak the truth and foster a sense of community among its audience. Their shows generated a public arena where it was possible to take a deep collective breath. When the band played "SOS," "Traumteufel," or "Alles wird besser," everyone in the crowd could feel the beating pulse of the present moment. In between songs, Tamara Danz spoke about the painful emptiness left behind by the mass exodus to the West, demanded a universal right to travel, and called on people to boycott GDR television, which had banned "Verlorene Kinder" from its playlists. Gorbachev button proudly on display, she revealed that she now liked having a Russian first name. In their persistent observation of Danz, the Stasi ascribed the singer a "vulgar and coarse" attitude, whose "supremely provocative" behavior "aimed at producing negative emotions and positions within younger audiences" (MfS 1989a, 119 and 116). The secret service identified Danz as one instigator of the sharpest and loudest appeal to come from artists that tumultuous fall, a resolution put out by prominent GDR rock musicians and songwriters on September 18, 1989, demanding a radical change of course from political leadership. The typewritten document, three-quarters of a page in length, began:

> We, the signatories of this letter, are concerned about the present state of our country, the mass exodus of many of our peers, the existential crises facing our social alternative, and the intolerable ignorance of state and party leadership, which trivializes the present contradictions and maintains a fixed course. It isn't about "reforms that will abolish Socialism," but reforms that will continue to make it viable in this country.

The statement staked out clear opposition to the West and upheld a leftist vision. No longer petitioners, the musicians stepped forward with heads held high:

> We urgently call for immediate public dialogue, here and now. We demand that the media open up to these issues. We demand a change to what are unbearable conditions. We want

> to address the present contradictions, since it is only through their resolution, not their trivialization, that a path through this crisis will be possible. Waiting cowardly to see provides pan-Germanist thinkers with arguments and premises. The time is ripe. If we do nothing, it will work against us! (Rauhut 1996, 291)

When the state declined to publish the resolution or otherwise engage in the dialogue that it called for, its authors began to read it from stage, breaking media silence around East Germany's plight and filling a vacuum left by the fatal triumphalist propaganda of the SED. The public responded enthusiastically and closed ranks, grateful for the flicker of hope it offered. The Stasi and political authorities meanwhile tried, ultimately in vain, to stop the "aggressively hostile resolution" (MfS 1989b), intimidating its defenders and applying pressure. Concerts were canceled, artists were banned from performing and received fines. As some of the first to sign the document, members of Silly received regular visits from the Stasi in an attempt to prevail upon the musicians, but they didn't give an inch. Tamara Danz recalled those turbulent weeks as a time of uncertain beginnings:

> Backstage was always total chaos after the concerts. Most people wanted to copy out the resolution or just get their political opinions off their chest for once. We also received an entire slew of letters, we were bombarded by questions. It was common from before for fans to want to know something about the music or the band—but that fall, it was really noticeable how many more people were looking to talk. (Danz 1990, interview)

Having the approval of the people "was something like a bulletproof vest" (Danz 1997a, 212).

After Tamara Danz read out the feared document a third time, Silly had the rest of its gigs canceled under flimsy pretexts: technical problems, broken pipes, and so on. Only once was there any straight talk, when the musicians received a telegram informing them that "as it is not currently foreseeable that the group Silly will revoke its declaration to read out the present resolution at its public events, we feel compelled to cancel the event planned for tomorrow" (Rommel 1989).

System Change

Silly could have followed in others' footsteps and steered clear of a risky boxing match with the state to focus on their careers in the West instead. Any number of doors stood open to the band, and all the right ingredients for success were present—talent, charisma, a touch of the exotic and, most importantly, a dazzling female lead. The band also had influential figures in the record industry, journalists, and promoters in its corner as friends and sympathizers. Yet the musicians lacked the willingness to compromise and conform needed to really take off. They would have had to sever their roots in the East and bow to the opportunistic rules of the free market. It wasn't something Silly was prepared to do. Fame and the temptations of the West couldn't bend them; they held to their identity as a GDR band. Thomas Stein, the head of Ariola at the time, remains impressed by their integrity today: "Tamara Danz, Ritchie Barton, Uwe Hassbecker all remain in my memory as people of high caliber. They stood by their word, a quality of commitment that unfortunately wasn't all too common then" (Stein 2023, interview).

Like every other GDR act Silly found itself confronted with existential challenges when the Wall came down. The state infrastructure of clubs and cultural venues imploded practically overnight, and government support for artists generally fell to the wayside. Finally able to see their international idols live in concert, few fans continued going to see GDR acts they knew well enough by now anyway. Making things more difficult still was the "artistic paralysis" that set in, in Tamara Danz's words (Heinze 1990, 11). When the state vanished, the "common enemy" (ibid.) vanished with it, an important antagonistic spur to creativity. Rock music ceased to function as a counterpublic sphere or alternative communicative space. Silly experienced this loss in meaning for themselves. Jim Rakete got at the crux of the matter: "With the fall of the Wall, the resistance that had given Silly its strength suddenly wasn't there. That was the elephant in the room. The opponent had left the ring" (Rakete 2023, interview).

Throughout the *Wende*, Tamara Danz could be found more frequently on talk shows than on stage. She was highly critical of reunification, warning against the GDR's annexation by West Germany. In late November 1989, she was among the first to sign "For our Country," a call-to-arms instigated by prominent East German intellectuals that protested against "our material and moral values being sold off" and called for "a socialist alternative to the Federal Republic" (Für unser Land 1989, 2). Later, the singer supported a "Call to Establish Committees for Justice," a proposed set of communal bodies aimed at protecting East Germans from being degraded to "second-class citizens" (Appell 1992, 1023). While acknowledging the imprint the GDR had made on her, Danz left no doubts about her rejection of dewy-eyed glorifications of the past. She advocated for an unsparing punishment of injustice and public access to the Stasi files, as well as exposing former top functionaries within the SED and the FDJ for contravening both law and morality by enriching themselves off nationally owned property.

The next Silly record—*Hurensöhne* (or *S.O.B.*), released in April 1993—revealed what had been preying on Danz's mind. This time she wrote a full three-quarters of all the lyrics, splitting the rest with Gerhard Gundermann. The most incendiary songs on the record came from Danz and didn't leave much to interpretation or imagination; the message was obvious. *Hurensöhne* is framed by two songs that get to grips with reunification. The opening track, "Halloween in Ostberlin" [Halloween in East Berlin], gives a sarcastic account of a merciless gold-rush atmosphere. In search of fresh blood, the "most ghoulish figures" fall upon a bleary-eyed East, divvying up pieces of the "new German cake" solely among themselves. Meanwhile, feeble-minded ex-GDR citizens are tranquilized with "junk" and "rotgut." "They clear it out all by themselves / the hovels and the bureaus / and we move on howling / off to the next party in the East / where a brawl's already raging / and we, the benign spirits / we even rip the shirts off their backs / just faster now and bolder." Yet beneath the razed surface, a rebellious seed still lies dormant. The marriage of East and West, "slut" and "hero" as they are described on the record's final track "Traumpaar" [Dream Couple], misleads us with a false image of harmony. "The fiery red hair / has all been done up in black / I have a sneaky feeling / it's going to grow back."

Hurensöhne was the last Silly album to feature explicitly political songs. The following record, *Paradies*, was received as a mature work about love and death. On July 22, 1996, just a few months after it came out, Tamara Danz died of cancer. Silly re-formed in 2006, recruiting actress Anna Loos to step in as singer. It turned out to be a brilliant strategic move. While Loos came from the East, she had gained national recognition as a film star, and her popularity gave Silly another shot at a Germany-wide career. When Loos departed after twelve years, the band's radius narrowed back again to the former East. Today, it is primarily fans born in the GDR and their children who make the pilgrimage to the band's shows to relive the warm sense of community, celebrate, and share in the memories. Silly remain dynamic, working with various guest vocalists, building new material into their shows and retrofitting old hits for the here and now. As a store of essential insights into the human condition, Silly's songs hold no expiration date and have kept their relevance for younger generations. The experiences of our present day still find reflection in their metaphors and poetry.

In the summer of 2023, I'm at a Silly show for the first time in a long while. I'm taken aback by the size of the audience and the number of young people in the crowd. The band opens the outdoor show with "Alles wird besser" off of *Februar*. Every last

Figure 7.1 *East Berlin, 1990: Silly perform at the defunct Stasi headquarters, in support of citizens who occupied the site to prevent files from being destroyed. Seen in the image are Tamara Danz and Uwe Hassbecker © Rolf Zoellner.*

word is just as relevant. We think of moral surrender in a world without hope, of war, greed, egotism, and our unstoppable race toward the abyss. "It's all getting better but it won't turn out well," goes the chorus. The crowd sings the lines right back, at the top of their voices.

Sources

Specialist Literature and Press

ADN. (1989). "Sich selbst aus unserer Gesellschaft ausgegrenzt." *Neues Deutschland,* October 2.

Ahbe, Thomas. (1997). "Ostalgie als Selbstermächtigung: Zur produktiven Stabilisierung ostdeutscher Identität." *Deutschland Archiv,* 30 (4): 614–19.

"Appell zur Gründung von Komitees für Gerechtigkeit vom 11. Juli 1992." (1992). *Blätter für deutsche und internationale Politik,* 37 (8): 1023–4.

Balitzki, Jürgen. (1989). "Connection: Sillys 'Februar' in München." *Journal für Unterhaltungskunst,* no. 4, pp. 28–29.

Bertram, Lutz. (1989). "Februar" [review]. *Journal für Unterhaltungskunst,* no. 3, pp. 38–39.

Bicher, Dietrich. (1989). "Silly-LP" [letter to the Editor]. *Sonntag,* May 7.

Böhme, Waltraud et al., ed. (1988). *Kleines politisches Wörterbuch,* 7th ed. Berlin (DDR): Dietz.

Covach, John. (2020). "Rock Historiography: Music, Artists, Perspectives, and Value." In *The Bloomsbury Handbook of Rock Music Research,* edited by Allan Moore and Paul Carr, 25–36. New York: Bloomsbury Academic.

Danz, Tamara. (1990). "Zum Stichwort Privilegien für Künstler in der DDR." *Berliner Zeitung,* November 29.

Danz, Tamara. (1997a). "Ein Höchstmaß an Freiheit: Das stürmische Jahr 89." In *Tamara Danz: Legenden*, edited by Alexander Osang, 209–14. Berlin: Ch. Links.

Danz, Tamara. (1997b). "Ein rollender Stein setzt kein Moos an: Die 'Gammler'-Jahre." In *Tamara Danz: Legenden*, edited by Alexander Osang, 205–6. Berlin: Ch. Links.

Dieckmann, Christoph. (1996). "Sie war von hier." *Die Zeit*, August 2.

Ebert, Horst et al., ed. (1975). *Wörterbuch zur sozialistischen Jugendpolitik*. Berlin (DDR): Dietz.

Eckermann, Johann Peter. (1916). *Gespräche mit Goethe in den letzten Jahren seines Lebens 1823–1832*. volume 2, edited by Eduard Castle. Berlin, Leipzig, Wien, Stuttgart: Deutsches Verlagshaus Bong & Co.

Frith, Simon. (1998). *Performing Rites: On the Value of Popular Music*. Cambridge, MA: Harvard University Press.

"Für unser Land." (1989). *Neues Deutschland*, November 29.

Green, Ben. (2018). "Popular Music in Mediated and Collective Memory." In *The Routledge Companion to Popular Music History and Heritage*, edited by Sarah Baker et al., 208–16. New York and London: Routledge.

Günter, Gabriele. (1989). "Noch nicht Frühling." *Junge Welt*, February 25/26.

Heinze, Waltraud. (1989). "Noch nicht Frühling." *Junge Welt*, February 25/26.

Heinze, Waltraud. (1990). "Rockmusik war immer ein Risiko: Die Befindlichkeiten der Tamara Danz" [interview]. *FF dabei*, no. 22.

Jachmann, Michael-Peter. (1989). "Silly-Fans mussten auf Hits nicht verzichten, doch hitverdächtiges war kaum zu hören." *Neuer Tag*, May 30.

Jacobus, Hans. (1987). "Wenn ich das Gefühl habe, die Arbeit hat sich gelohnt…" [interview]. *FF dabei*, no. 24.

Karma, Werner. (1997). "Abschiedsbrief an meine tote Freundin." In *Tamara Danz: Legenden*, edited by Alexander Osang, 215–22. Berlin: Ch. Links.

Karma, Werner. (2002). "Halbzeit für Insulaner." In *Alles wird besser, nichts wird gut: Alte und neue Songtexte 1976–2001*, edited by Werner Karma, 293–334. Berlin: Schwarzkopf & Schwarzkopf.

Karma, Werner. (2021). "Sonnenblumen (für Tamara)." In *Paradiesvögel fängt man nicht ein: Hommage an Tamara Danz*, edited by Wolfgang Martin, 59–79. Berlin: Bild und Heimat.

Könau, Steffen. (2024). "Lieder vom letzten Winter." *Mitteldeutsche Zeitung*, weekend supplement, February 24/25.

Lahann, Birgit. (1989). "Glasnost nach Noten." *Stern*, March 30.

Lambertsen, Jakob. (1987). "Skanderborgs smukkeste Danz." *Jyllands-Posten*, August 10.

Lange, Wolfgang. (1983). "Silly: Mont Klamott" [review]. *Melodie und Rhythmus*, no. 7, p. 2.

Lange, Wolfgang. (1989). "Februar" [review]. *Melodie und Rhythmus*, no. 2, p. 13.

Löhr, Albrecht. (1989). "Silly-LP" [letter to the Editor]. *Sonntag*, May 14.

Marx, Karl, and Friedrich Engels. (1974). *The Communist Manifesto*. Harmondsworth: Penguin Books.

Osang, Alexander. (1995). "Eines Tages wollte Grigori Egon Krenz verbrennen." *Berliner Zeitung*, April 28.

Osang, Alexander. (1997). *Tamara Danz: Legenden*. Berlin: Ch. Links.

Oschmann, Dirk. (2023). *Der Osten: eine westdeutsche Erfindung*, 7th ed. Berlin: Ullstein.

Pekacz, Jolanta. (1994). "Did Rock Smash the Wall? The Role of Rock in Political Transition." *Popular Music*, 13 (1): 41–9.

Pilz, Michael. (2010). "Silly sind endlich in Deutschland angekommen." *Die Welt*, August 28.

Plato. (2008). *Republic.* Translated by Robin Waterfield. Oxford: Oxford University Press.

Rauhut, Michael. (1996). *Schalmei und Lederjacke: Udo Lindenberg, BAP, Underground – Rock und Politik in den achtziger Jahren.* Berlin: Schwarzkopf & Schwarzkopf.

Rauhut, Michael. (2002). *Rock in der DDR 1964 bis 1989.* Bonn: Bundeszentrale für politische Bildung.

Rauhut, Michael. (2023). "Meuterei auf der Titanic: Die ostdeutsche Rockband Silly emanzipierte das Ich vom Wir." In *Vom Ich zum Wir und wieder zurück? Subjektverständnisse zwischen Politisierung und Entradikalisierung seit den 1960er Jahren,* edited by Knud Andresen, Sebastian Justke, and Stefanie Schüler-Springorum, 120–39. Göttingen: Wallstein.

Rauhut, Michael, and Beate Peter. (2021). "Small Cracks, Complex Structures: Trends and Traditions in the Historiography of the GDR's Popular Music." *Popular Music History,* 14 (2): 97–105.

Schmidtendorf, Hermann. (1986). "Geballte Faust beim Liebeswalzer." *Die Welt,* November 20.

Scholz, Martin. (1989). "Texte vom Baggerfahrer." *Frankfurter Rundschau,* April 15.

Schulz, Jürgen. (1987). "Jahrelang über die Dörfer getingelt." *Vorwärts,* April 25.

Stolle, Ralph. (1993). "Man muss auch bescheuerte Mehrheiten akzeptieren" [interview]. *Junge Welt,* April 14.

Thomas, Ilona. (1989). "Amigas außergewöhnliche Angebote." *Berliner Zeitung,* March 18/19.

Tiger, Eli. (1989). "Silly holte die Fans delikat aus der Reserve." *Berliner Morgenpost,* April 13.

Treitler, Leo. (2001). "The Historiography of Music: Issues of Past and Present." In *Rethinking Music,* edited by Nicholas Cook and Mark Everist, 356–77. Oxford: Oxford University Press.

"Verfassung der Deutschen Demokratischen Republik vom 6. April 1968." (1984). In *Verfassung der Deutschen Demokratischen Republik und Jugendgesetz,* 10th ed., 5–37. Berlin (DDR): Staatsverlag der DDR.

Wicke, Peter. (1987). *Anatomie des Rock.* Leipzig: VEB Deutscher Verlag für Musik.

Wicke, Peter. (1992). "The Times They Are A-Changin': Rock Music and Political Change in East Germany." In *Rockin' the Boat: Mass Music and Mass Movements,* edited by Reebee Garofalo, 81–92. Boston: South End Press.

Wicke, Peter. (1996). "Zwischen Förderung und Reglementierung: Rockmusik im System der DDR-Kulturbürokratie." In *Rockmusik und Politik: Analysen, Interviews und Dokumente,* edited by Peter Wicke and Lothar Müller, 11–27. Berlin: Ch. Links.

Archival Documents and Gray Literature

BMG Ariola. (1989). *Silly: Februar* [press kit]. Munich.

Czerny, Peter, Generaldirektor, Generaldirektion beim Komitee für Unterhaltungskunst. (1980). *Informationen zur Gruppe "Familie Silly".* October 30. BArch, DR 1/26936.

Erber, Gabriele. (1988). *Fans in der Rockmusik: Aspekte einer aktiven Wirklichkeitsbewältigung im sozialen Gebrauch von Rockmusik durch Jugendliche in der DDR.* PhD diss., Humboldt-Universität zu Berlin.

Familie Silly. (1981). *Letter to Kurt Hager.* April 29. BArch, DY 30/27370.

Familie Silly. (1982). *Letter to Kurt Hager.* September 13. BArch, DY 30/27370.

Generaldirektion beim Komitee für Unterhaltungskunst. (1984). *Standpunkt zur Entwicklung der Rockmusik in der DDR*. May 21. BArch, DY 30/27376.

Hager, Kurt. 1983 [typewritten note]. February 3. BArch, DY 30/27370.

Leitner, Olaf. (1989). *Das Reisen dämpft die Illusionen: Porträt der Rockgruppe Silly*. RIAS broadcast from March 26 [transcript]. Copy of the document in author's possession.

MfS. (1966). *Dienstanweisung Nr. 4/66 zur politisch-operativen Bekämpfung der politisch-ideologischen Diversion und Untergrundtätigkeit unter jugendlichen Personenkreisen in der DDR*. May 15. 24–51. BArch, MfS, ZA, MfS VVS 008–365/66.

MfS, BV Berlin. (1980) [telex message]. October 20. 58. BArch, MfS, HA XX, 15826.

MfS, HA XX, to BV Berlin, Abt. XX. (1981). *Danz, Tamara – Sängerin in der Gruppe „Familie Silly"*. March 16. 65. BArch, MfS, HA XX, 15826.

MfS, BV Berlin, Abt. XX, to MfS, HA XX. (1984). *Reisefähigkeit von Tamara Danz*. November 9. 116. BArch, MfS, HA XX, 15826.

MfS. (1985). *Tamara Danz*. 143. BArch, MfS, HA XX/AKG RK, Nr. 29650–29685.

MfS, HA II. (1987). *Information: Aktuelle Situation im Komitee für Unterhaltungskunst*. March 16. 288. BArch, MfS, BV Berlin, Abt. XX, Nr. 9155.

MfS, KD Berlin-Weißensee. (1989a). *Information zu den Veranstaltungen "Rock in Weißensee" am 13. und 14.05.1989*. May 15. 116–19. BArch, MfS, HA XX, 12413.

MfS. (1989b) [handwritten note]. September 20. 1. BArch, MfS, HA XX, ZMA 2109.

Ministerium für Kultur. (1987). *Betr.: Entwicklung der Gruppe "Silly"*. BArch, DR 1/26936.

Ministerrat der DDR. (1982). *Anordnung über die Auswahl, Bestätigung und Vorbereitung von Reise- und Auslandskadern und die Durchführung ihrer dienstlichen Reisen.* January 13. 1–39. BArch, MfS, BdL, Dok. 003846.

Richter, Claus. (1988). *Porträt der Rockgruppe Silly.* ARD broadcast from September 5 [transcript]. 139–44. BArch, MfS, HA XX, 15826.

Rommel, Direktor Bezirkskonzert Suhl. (1989). *Veranstaltung am 17.10.1989* [telegram]. Copy of the document in author's possession.

Rundfunk der DDR, Hauptabteilung Musik. (1976). *Konzeption der Lektoratsarbeit der Produktionsabteilung Tanzmusik.* July 14. DRA, KV 38/76.

Rundfunk der DDR, Produktionsabteilung Tanzmusik. (1981). *Lektorat am 7.9.1981* [minutes]. DRA, HA Musik/Abt. TM 1981.

Rundfunk der DDR, Produktionsabteilung Tanzmusik. (1982). *Zu Rocktexten, die in den letzten Monaten abgelehnt wurden.* November 17. DRA, HA Musik/1982.

Steineckert, Gisela. (1984a). *Letter to Hans-Joachim Hoffmann.* October 23. BArch, DR 1/26915.

Steineckert, Gisela. (1984b). *Letter to Hans-Joachim Hoffmann.* November 5. BArch, DR 1/26915.

Voos, Gabriele. (1985). *Rockmusik im sozialen Gebrauch Jugendlicher: Eine Analyse der Fanpost der DDR-Rockgruppe Silly.* Diploma thesis, Humboldt-Universität zu Berlin.

Zabel, Bodo. (1989a). *Hausmitteilung an den Minister für Kultur.* April 4. BArch, MfS, HA XX, 15826.

Zabel, Bodo, Leiter Abteilung Unterhaltungskunst, Ministerium für Kultur. (1989b). *Aktennotiz.* August 11. BArch, DR 1/19380.

Zentralrat der FDJ. (1985). *Reisebericht zur Entsendung der Gruppe Silly zum Laulu-Festival vom 30.5. bis 4.6.1985 nach Helsinki.* Copy of the document in author's possession.

ZK der SED, Abteilung Kultur. (1982). *Hinweise zu einigen aktuellen Erscheinungen der Entwicklung der Rockmusik in der DDR*. Copy of the document in author's possession.

ZK der SED. (1983). *Hausmitteilung*. April 18. BArch, DY 30/23055.

Discography

Silly. (1980). *Rocktopus*. 202814-320.

Familie Silly. (1981). *Tanzt keiner Boogie?* Amiga 855778.

Silly. (1982). "Die Gräfin" c/w "Dicke Luft". Amiga 456513.

Silly. (1983). *Mont Klamott*. Amiga 855972.

Silly. (1985). Liebeswalzer. Amiga 856069.

Silly. (1986). *Bataillon d'Amour*. Amiga 856195.

Silly. (1989). *Februar*. Ariola 209563.

Silly. (1989). *Februar*. Amiga 856316.

Silly. (1993). *Hurensöhne*. DSB 3065-2.

Silly. (1996). *Paradies*. SPV Recordings 085-89982.

Interviews

Danz, Tamara, lead singer of Silly, May 8, 1990.

Heilmann, David, recording engineer, Preußen Tonstudio, January 30, 2024.

Hentschel, Christian, founder of the first Silly fan club, September 28, 2023.

Hoffmann, Uwe, producer, March 1, 2024.

Karma, Werner, lyricist, September 20, 2023.

Ortlepp, Dieter, audio engineer, Amiga, January 31, 2024.

Rakete, Jim, manager, producer, photographer, September 22, 2023.
Silly: Ritchie Barton, Uwe Hassbecker, Jäcki Reznicek, September 18, 2023.
Schmidt-André, Jürgen, graphic designer, July 4, 2023.
Stein, Thomas, CEO BMG Ariola, October 12, 2023.

Index